THE HITCHHIKER'S GUIDE TO MARS

THE HITCHHIKER'S GUIDE TO MARS

ELON MUSK AND THE 42 PRINCIPLES FOR LIFE

MACK MODERIE

The Hitchhiker's Guide to Mars
Elon Musk and the 42 Principles for Life

ISBN:
Paperback: 979-8-9882581-0-0
Hardcover: 979-8-9882581-5-5
eBook: 979-8-9882581-1-7

Editor: Ellen Fishbein
Jacket design: Ben LaCour
Cover and sketch (within book) image:
Photo by Jurvetson on Flickr

FOR MY FATHER AND MOTHER.
THANK YOU FOR ALL THAT
YOU HAVE GIVEN.

CONTENTS

THINGS TO KEEP IN MIND (DISCLAIMER)

This book is a collection of Elon Musk's wisdom over the years. These quotes were not said or written for this book. So, I've structured the book into what I hope proves to be an optimal learning format. I've done my best to group Musk's quotes based on 42 actionable Principles. At the end of each section, I've included an example (a.k.a. "Application") from Musk's life to cement the Principle and its relevance further. I am in no way intending to detract from Musk's own words through my own but have simply built what I thought would be most useful to people. Here are several important points:

- Musk's direct words are indicated by quotation marks.

- Some quotes, specifically the longer ones, have been edited slightly for clarity.

- In writing this book, I may have mistakenly interpreted, misunderstood, or inaccurately re-contextualized things. I made every effort to provide the original intent of Musk's words.

- The words in the Principle and Application sections are mostly my own. I could have easily thrown hundreds of quotes into this book and separated them into broad categories, but I thought that was too boring. I wanted to build something unique that might provoke thought and discussion.

- Not every quote was obtained through a primary source. However, I made a significant effort (and I mean hundreds of hours) to ensure that all quotes came from reputable sources. I've cited sources for every quote in this book. I have not put a single quote into this book that I didn't feel was legitimate.

- I have not used in-text citations with Musk's quotes because it seemed to distract from what's most important: the ideas. Academic-style citations interrupt the flow of knowledge, in my opinion. If you want to know the source of the quote so that you may watch, read, or listen to Musk, you can find the source easily in the back of the book.

- I imagine that Musk will at some point change his mind on some of the topics housed in this book. For this reason, I have aspired to focus on including time-less wisdom alone. Please keep in mind that if you are reading this in the future, what is written in this book may need adjusting.

- Some quotes are straight from Musk's Twitter account, and he uses brevity online.

- I have purposefully kept my brackets containing context/information out of Musk's quotes to keep the words pure and uninterrupted. I also use brevity in the brackets purposefully.

- There are words in this book which are capitalized, like Civilization, Consciousness, Empire, Narrative etc. This is done on purpose.

- Elon Musk isn't earning any money from this book.

Simplicity, especially in language, was at the top of my mind as I was writing this book. The first draft included a lot of technical quotes and content; however, it quickly became obvious to me that, although some would appreciate the nature of that kind of a work, it wouldn't be optimal. So, I've tried to distill information as best as possible and make things simple.

The Principles in this book aren't ironclad "rules" that you need to follow 24/7/365. There will be times when the Principles should be applied and times when they shouldn't. Think of this list of Principles like a toolkit: mental models that you can access when you need them. It's up to you to learn when to use these tools. I hope you think the ideas over, imagining future scenarios and considering how they may apply to your own unique position in life.

Many of these Principles relate to one another and overlap. Certain concepts are repeated. However, everything in this book was written deliberately (the order of the Principles, the language used, the formatting of the pages, etc.).

Finally, knowledge is derivative to some degree. Did Musk extract all of this wisdom from the ether? No. Some ideas are relatively personal, and some came from other people. But the important aspect here, in my view, is that these Principles are working for Musk. They're not untested. They're Principles that yield results in the real world, as Musk has shown through the results he's gotten over the years. At least that's how I see it.

I wrote most of this book in the second person—addressing "you," the reader. It's important to remember that "you" includes me, the writer. Everything here applies to me as much as to anyone else.

THIS ONE'S FOR YOU, MY LEADERS

This one's for you, my leaders: I can see
in you the strength to topple tyranny,
to carry those who travel wearily,
to grapple monstrous Chaos in its tracks,
to lift oppressors off their victims' backs,
to open minds & hearts & avenues
to know & love the truth so much abused—
& even this weird year,
I see
in you
the vision that beholds the future's torch;
it's in your reach—believe it!   you are free
to take that torch, and march it to the sea.

From *Spacefaring* by Ellen Fishbein

INTRODUCTION

WHAT IS THIS BOOK?

I am building a collection of Elon Musk's wisdom and knowledge. Generally speaking, I believe those who do what others cannot do are able to do so because they know what others do not know. Lack of knowledge is a huge barrier to getting results in life. So, my intention was to know more of what Musk knows and share that knowledge in an interesting and digestible form.

WHY WAS THIS BOOK WRITTEN?

In my reading, I've noticed a trend among influential people: they always read and learn about the great people who came before them. I started to think: if my intention is to have a significant positive impact on the world, who better to study than Elon Musk? Studying Musk has had an incredible impact on my life across the board. In light of that, I wanted to share with others what I've learned and to build the resource I wish had been available to me.

    I also wanted to give back. One thing Musk doesn't have time for is writing books. Musk said so himself: "I am primarily trying to advance two causes: sustainable energy & extending life/consciousness beyond Earth. There is also the existential threat of AI, which we should aspire to mitigate. This doesn't leave time to write books."

I thought that this book could be a way I could give back to Musk and hopefully help as many others as humanly possible in the process.

HOW WAS THIS BOOK WRITTEN?

I started by imagining the future. I imagined what it might be like to visit a library or archive in some future Civilization. I imagined I would sit down and begin typing, speaking, or 'neuralinking' into a screen or hologram, accessing the profile of Elon Musk in a futuristic encyclopedia, like Isaac Asimov's *Encyclopædia Galactica*. I'd scroll to a "Principles for Life" section, in which I could see a list of useful life lessons the encyclopedists had gleaned from this historical figure. These Principles would showcase his own words (quotes) and also provide examples from his life that reinforce the ideas. This section of Musk's futuristic profile would be a distillation of priceless wisdom gathered over the course of an astounding life. I wrote the book with this future in mind.

HERE'S HOW EACH SECTION IS LAID OUT:

TITLE: A few words describing the big idea.

PRINCIPLE: The principle in the form of an actionable sentence, plus a few more lines summarizing the principle. (By the way, here's the definition of "principle": a fundamental truth that serves as the foundation for a system of belief or behavior or for a chain of reasoning).

QUOTES: Relevant and insightful quotes. I primarily collected these quotes from interviews, books, and Musk's Twitter account.

APPLICATION: A practical discussion of how someone might apply the principle, including further context and examples from Musk's life to help cement the ideas.

OVERVIEW OF ELON MUSK

1970s

South Africa: Musk was born in Pretoria, South Africa on June 28, 1971. He spent his entire childhood in South Africa. He could often be found reading books, riding motorbikes, or programming computers. However, he wasn't destined to stay in South Africa. Instead, he applied for Canadian citizenship after high school. While he waited for his Canadian citizenship, Musk briefly attended the University of Pretoria.

1980s

Canada: Upon arriving in Canada in 1989, Musk worked a series of odd jobs while living with relatives. After a brief stint with his extended family, he attended Queen's University in Kingston, Ontario.

1990s

America: Musk transferred to the University of Pennsylvania on scholarship in 1992. He acquired dual bachelor's degrees in physics and economics.

Zip2: In 1995, Musk moved to California to pursue a PhD at Stanford University. After two days, he dropped out to pursue an internet startup with his brother Kimbal Musk. They built Zip2, which was an online city guide software company. Compaq acquired Zip2 in 1999 for $307 million. Musk made $22 million.

2000s

PayPal: Right after the sale of Zip2, Musk co-founded a company called X.com. X.com was an internet finance and money-transfer startup. In 2000, X.com merged with Confinity. The company was then renamed PayPal and was acquired by eBay in 2002 for $1.5 billion. Musk made $180 million.

SpaceX: With the money Musk made from the sale of PayPal, he founded Space Exploration Technologies Corporation (a.k.a. "SpaceX") in 2002. SpaceX is a spaceflight services company created with the ultimate intention of helping to make life multi-planetary. SpaceX has made tremendous progress on this mission over the years—winning contracts, servicing the International Space Station with supplies and people, landing first-stage boosters, launching more rockets than any other company or organization... the list goes on. Today, they are building Starship, the vehicle intended to take us to Mars. Also, SpaceX has developed a satellite internet constellation called Starlink. Starlink was created in 2019 and has already played a significant role in providing internet to rural areas of the world.

Tesla: The founding and early days of Tesla are often considered controversial. So, I will include Musk's own words on the matter:

"The actual origin of Tesla goes back to 2003, when I had lunch with JB [Straubel] in El Segundo and we got to talking about electric cars and JB said: 'Hey, have you tried the AC propulsion tzero?' I said: 'No.' But we talked about battery technology and how the lithium ion would enable a long-range car. I'd never heard of Eberhard at this point—never heard of him. So, then I got a test drive from AC Propulsion's tzero, and I was like: 'Wow, OK, this is pretty cool.' At first, I was just like, 'Well, can you guys just make me a tzero, I'll buy one from you...' they didn't want to make another one..."

When Musk gave up on working with AC Propulsion, he got connected with a new group of guys who were interested in commercializing an electric car. In the same interview:

"The first group I met was Eberhard, Tarpenning and Wright. Eberhard keeps trying to erase Ian Wright from history as well because they hate each other... There were no employees, there were no offices, there was no IP, there was no nothing—literally nothing. There was nothing you would call a company... There was an empty shell corporation that had zero value... except the general idea of commercializing the tzero, which I had before meeting them. Like, if I had not met them I would have just moved forward, created a company with JB, commercialized the tzero and gone our way... and that's actually what happened at the end of the day—except with a lot of grief along the way... the key point here is that... the money I provided was the least important thing that I provided to the company. There was no company. And if I had not met them, I would have just moved forward and created Tesla, and I think it would be indistinguishable from what it is today... I think we could have avoided a lot of drama as well in the early days."

Tesla has produced the original Roadster, Model S, Model X, Model 3, Model Y, and Semi and will be delivering the Cybertruck soon as well. Tesla also plays a crucial role in solar/battery technology (Tesla acquired Solar City in 2016, which Musk also played a role in creating). Tesla is currently experiencing tremendous success and is more or less the reason the electric vehicle industry came back to life.

2010s

OpenAI: Musk co-founded OpenAI in 2015. It was originally a nonprofit organization created to democratize and safely develop AI technology. However, Musk resigned from the board in 2018 due to potential conflicts of interest with Tesla's own AI work. The company has since transformed from a nonprofit to a for-profit corporation. OpenAI released ChatGPT in 2022, and it has taken the internet by storm.

Neuralink: Musk co-founded Neuralink in 2016. The company's mission is to advance brain-machine interfaces and ultimately safeguard against the dangers of artificial intelligence. They have been making interesting progress in terms of their results with animals. For example, they have been able to get a monkey to play Pong, a video game, with its mind.

The Boring Company: This company was also founded by Musk in 2016. The Boring Company was created in an effort to eradicate "soul-destroying" traffic. Their aim was to build tunnels to aid the inefficient traffic system. They have announced a number of public projects and currently run a fully operational tunnel under Las Vegas, NV.

2020s

Twitter: Most recently, Musk bought Twitter in 2022. He intends to create a free speech platform that is maximally trusted and functions as a sort of digital town square. The app has a long way to go in order to be turned around. However, significant progress has been made already, and overall, things are headed in a positive direction considering the user growth it has accumulated since the takeover.

Quite an exciting life,⌀ and it just gets more interesting as the years pass!

⌀ Obviously, this is a brief overview. However, my intention in including this timeline was to simply give a short summary of Musk to those who are unfamiliar. There are plenty of resources out there to learn about Musk's life, but documenting his life story in detail wasn't the goal of this book.

"I swear my responsibility to the highest good for consciousness, while always re-examining what the highest good is."

| Elon Musk

THE 42 PRINCIPLES

1. FEEDBACK LOOPS

PRINCIPLE:

RUN AND OPTIMIZE A FEEDBACK LOOP IN YOUR MIND.

Gather experiences and information, collect people's input, think it over, and take action to improve your output. Repeat.

QUOTES:

"I think it's very important to have a feedback loop, where you're constantly thinking about what you've done and how you could be doing it better. I think that's the single best piece of advice—constantly think about how you could be doing things better and questioning yourself."

—

"One of the biggest challenges I think is making sure you have a corrective feedback loop, and then maintaining that corrective feedback loop over time even when people want to tell you exactly what you want to hear…"

—

Interviewer (Kevin Rose): "Where do you do that [seek negative feedback]?"

Musk: "Everyone I talk to, in fact, when friends get a product, I say: 'Look, don't tell me what you like, tell me what you don't like.' Because otherwise your friend is not going to tell you what he doesn't like, he's gonna say: 'Oh, I love this and that' and leave out the 'This is the stuff I don't like list' because he wants to be your friend and doesn't want to offend you. So, you really need to sort of coax negative feedback, and you know that if somebody is your friend or at least not your enemy and they're giving you negative feedback, then they may be wrong but it's coming from a good place, and sometimes even your enemies could give you good negative feedback… People should just view positive feedback like water off a duck's back, you know, really underweight that and overweight negative feedback."

—

"I think it's very important to actively seek out and listen very carefully to negative feedback. This is something that people tend to avoid because it's painful, but I think this is a very common mistake—to not actively seek out and listen to negative feedback."

—

"Start somewhere and then really be prepared to question your assumptions, fix what you did wrong, and adapt to reality."

—Elon Musk

APPLICATION:

A feedback loop is a process by which you incorporate new information into your actions to improve your output. If your feedback loop is working well, when you put something out there (such as a product or an idea), you can quickly receive new information that will help you improve the next version.

There are a few different flavors of feedback loops. In some cases, you can create your own feedback loop by documenting your observations about your output and then adjusting your inputs based on what you've observed. For example, imagine you're trying to maximize the flight time of your videography drone on a single charge. You can try iterating on your design after observing how much power each design uses. You might not need any other human beings to execute this feedback loop.

Musk is constantly using his own mental feedback loops

to iterate and course-correct. At Tesla, he's heavily involved in vehicle design and production. He has spent time optimizing his way of collecting observations. In the factory, he gathers personal observations about the car, thinks things over, and then makes adjustments to the vehicle. He describes his process like this:

> "You can train yourself to pay attention to the tiny details; I think almost anyone can. Although this is very much a double-edged sword because then you see all the little details, and little things drive you crazy. Most people don't consciously see the small details, but they do subconsciously see them. Your mind takes in an overall impression, and you know if something is appealing or not even though you may not be able to point out exactly why. It's a summation of these many small details... You can make yourself pay attention to... essentially to bring the subconscious awareness into conscious awareness... Just pay really close attention... Look closely and carefully."

Musk is describing a personal feedback loop that happens mostly in his mind. In many cases, though, his feedback loops involve many other people. For example, Tesla constantly improves its internal processes through feedback loops within the organization:

> "I also believe in having a tight feedback loop between engineering and production. If production is far away from engineering, you lose that feedback loop. So, someone who designed the car in a particular way

doesn't realize that it's very difficult to manufacture in the particular way that it's designed. But if the factory floor is 50 feet away from their desk, then they can just go out and they can just see it. It's obvious. And they can have a dialogue with the people on the floor. And likewise, a lot of the people on the manufacturing team have great ideas about how to improve the car, but if they're far away, they can't communicate that to the engineers who designed it. I think that is something that's often neglected but having that strong bi-directional feedback loop between engineering and production is really helpful for making the car better, finding efficiencies, and lowering the cost."

Even more broadly, Musk uses the internet to source feedback from large numbers of people from all over the world. He's constantly getting feedback from the Tesla community in particular—people share their thoughts and concerns all the time, and Musk listens. Tesla has made countless adjustments to its cars based on customers' Tweets. It doesn't stop at Tesla, either; Musk interacts with YouTube channels dedicated to space exploration, to relevant non-profit clubs, and to social media accounts that share his quotes...

Musk University (me): "I would like to write a book on Elon's wisdom and knowledge.

Would this book be useful to you?"

Musk: "Yes"

Musk doesn't shy away from any amount of public opinion

or criticism—he says: "A well-thought-out critique of whatever you're doing is as valuable as gold and you should seek that from everyone you can."

By putting aside his ego, Musk collects all of the information produced by his supporters (and critics, too). With this information, he can do far more than he ever could if he were limited to his own observations.

Last but not least, Musk's Twitter takeover is another example of a feedback loop that's worth including here. He recently bought the company and has been moving with an extreme sense of urgency stemming from a desire to avoid bankruptcy. The company has been on the brink of bankruptcy for years, and unless it's rebuilt, it will die. Since the acquisition, people from all walks of life have been taking time to collect and write their thoughts on how Twitter can improve. What's even more incredible is that Musk reads a ton of them—and interacts with these individuals publicly. Where else have you seen anything like this? There aren't any popular CEOs personally asking how their app can be improved on that same app… and then taking all suggestions into consideration publicly. But Musk literally tweeted: "Complaint hotline operator online! Please mention your complaints below."

At the time of this writing, Musk is in full innovation mode—keeping what works and amplifying it and deleting what doesn't work. It is cool to see him build in real time. In many ways, it is a masterclass on rapid innovation. If you pay close enough attention on Twitter today, you can see Musk's cumulative knowledge from building SpaceX and Tesla being put into action with this Twitter project.

Practical side note: I hope to iterate on this book. If you have feedback on any part of it, please help me by sharing your feedback via this email:

muskuniversityfeedback@gmail.com

2. TAKE ACTION

PRINCIPLE:

JUST TAKE ACTION.

No matter how much you know, it's useless if you don't act on it. Humanity's future depends upon those who take action.

QUOTES:

> **Chris Anderson, TEDx:** "There's a whole generation coming through who seem really sad about the future. What would you say to them?"
>
> **Musk:** "Well, I think if you want the future to be good, you must make it so. Take action to make it good and it will be."

—

"People sometimes think technology just automatically gets better every year, but it actually doesn't; it only gets better if smart people work like crazy to make it better. That's how any technology actually gets better. And by itself, technology, if people don't work at it, it actually will decline. I mean if you look at the history of civilizations, many civilizations... look at, say, Ancient Egypt, where they were able to build these incredible pyramids, and they basically forgot how to build pyramids. And even hieroglyphics, they forgot how to read hieroglyphics, or you look at Rome, and how they were able to build these incredible roadways and aqueducts and indoor plumbing, and then they forgot how to do all those things. And there are many such examples in history. So, I think just be sure to bear in mind that, you know, entropy is not on your side."

—

"I don't spend my time pontificating about high-concept things; I spend my time solving engineering and manufacturing problems."

—

"My background educationally is physics and economics, and I grew up in sort of an engineering environment—my father is an electromechanical engineer. And so, there were lots of engineering things around me. When I asked for an explanation,

I got the true explanation of how things work. I also did things like make model rockets, and in South Africa there were no pre-made rockets; I had to go to the chemist and get the ingredients for rocket fuel, mix it, and put it in a pipe."

———

"I could either watch it happen or be a part of it."

—Elon Musk

APPLICATION:

Musk has always been a man of action. Even from the very beginning, Musk didn't shy away from making an effort to realize his dreams:

> "The reason I came out to Stanford was actually to work on energy storage technologies for electric cars. That summer of '95, I was looking at the internet and it seemed to me like the internet was going to have a big effect on humanity. So, I thought, well, I can either work on electric vehicle technology and do my PhD at Stanford, and watch the internet get built, or I could put my studies on hold and try to be part of the internet. At first, I tried to get a job at Netscape, because that was the only internet company, and they didn't respond to me. So, I was like, 'OK, if I can't get a job at the only internet company, then I'd better try starting something.' But I talked to my professor, and

I said: 'Look, I'm gonna try starting a company; it's probably not going to succeed and if it doesn't succeed, can I come back?' And he said: 'Sure, no problem' and so I put my studies on hold and I started the company."

Most people don't abandon their studies in pursuit of their dreams. Even fewer people would choose to start their own business after failing to find a job in their desired industry. But it all starts with taking action—doing the thing that you know, deep down, needs to be done.

3. FIRST PRINCIPLES

PRINCIPLE:

START FROM FIRST PRINCIPLES.

Whenever possible, reason from first principles. Boil things down to the most fundamental truths. Get down to bedrock: find the principles that aren't built on any other principles or assumptions. Find the axioms that won't change. Avoid using conventional wisdom, which consists of thoughts like "This is how it will always be, because this is how it's always been." Assuming that things will continue to be the same as they've always been—without questioning whether the Laws of Nature dictate that things must be like that—is the path to an average future that isn't any different from the past.

QUOTES:

"Physics is the law; everything else is a recommendation. I've met a lot of people who can break the law but never met anyone who can break physics.

So, for any kind of technology problem you have to make sure you're not violating physics. First principles analysis I think is something that can be applied to any walk of life; it's really just saying: 'Let's boil something down to the most fundamental principles, the things that we are most confident are true at a foundational level and that sets your axiomatic base. Then you reason up from there and then you cross-check your conclusion against the axiomatic truths… Another good physics tool is thinking about things in the limit. If you take a particular thing and you scale it to a very large number or to a very small number, how do things change?… Like manufacturing, which I think is just a very underrated problem… So, let's say… you are trying to figure out… why is this part or product expensive? Is it because of something fundamentally foolish that we're doing or is it because our volume is too low? So, then you say, 'OK, what if our volume was a million units a year, is it still expensive?' If it's still expensive at a million units a year, then volume is not the reason why your thing is expensive, there's something fundamental about the design… Then you have to change the design or part to something that is not fundamentally expensive."

—

"Don't just follow the trend; you may have heard me say that it's good to think in terms of the physics approach of first principles, which is: rather than reasoning by analogy, you boil things down to the most fundamental truths you can imagine, and you reason up from there. This is a good way to figure out if something really makes sense or if it's just what everybody else is doing. It's hard to think that way. You can't think that way about everything; it takes a lot of effort. But if you're trying to do something new, it's the best way to think."

—

"With regard to tools for understanding the world, I think the physics framework is extremely helpful. In physics, they call it thinking from a first principles standpoint, where you try to understand the most fundamental truths in a particular situation and reason up from there and then you test your conclusions against what you believe to be the fundamental truths. So, in physics, it would be like testing to see if you're violating conservation of energy or conservation of momentum or something like that. And then constantly trying to be less wrong. You should always assume that you're to some degree wrong, and you want to be less wrong. This is, I think, very important."

—

"I think generally people's thinking process is too bound by convention or analogy to prior experiences. It's rare that people try to think of something on a first principles basis. They'll say: 'We'll do that because it's always been done that way.' Or they'll not do it because 'Well, nobody's ever done that, so it must not be good.' But that's just a ridiculous way to think. You have to build the reasoning from the ground up, from the first principles, which is the phrase that's used in physics. You look at the fundamentals and construct your reasoning from that, and then you see if you have a conclusion that works or doesn't work, and it may or may not be different from what people have done in the past."

—

"I started reading a lot of books on rockets and did sort of a first principles analysis of a rocket, just broke down the materials that are in a rocket— what would it cost to buy those materials versus the price of the rocket and there's a gigantic difference between the raw material cost of the rocket and the finished cost of the rocket. So, there must be something wrong happening in going from the con- stituent atoms to the final shape, and I found that to certainly be true."

—

"I said, 'OK, let's look at the first principles. What is a rocket made out of? Aerospace-grade alumi- num alloys, plus some titanium, copper, and carbon fiber.' And then I asked: 'What is the value of those materials on the commodity market?' It turned out that the materials cost of a rocket was around 2% of the typical price—which is a crazy ratio for a large mechanical product.'"

———

"I do kind of feel like my head is full! My context-switching penalty is high, and my process isolation is not what it used to be. Frankly though, I think most people can learn a lot more than they think they can. They sell themselves short without trying. One bit of advice: it is important to view knowledge as sort of a semantic tree—make sure you understand the fundamental principles, i.e., the trunk and big branches, before you get into the leaves/details or there's nothing for them to hang on to."

—Elon Musk

APPLICATION:

Tesla's innovation on the battery front exemplifies first-principles thinking:

"Somebody could say, in fact people do, 'Battery packs are really expensive and that's just the way they will always be because that's the way they've been in the past.' No, that's pretty dumb. Because if you apply that reasoning to anything new, you wouldn't be able to ever get to that new thing. You know, you can't say: 'Nobody wants a car because horses are great and we're used to them, they can eat grass, there's lots of grass all over the place, there's no gasoline for people to buy—so people are never going to get cars.' People did say that. And for batteries they would say: 'Historically it's cost $600 per kilowatt-hour, so it's not going to be much better than that in the future.' No, you have to say: 'What are the batteries made of?' First principles would be: 'What are the material constituents of the batteries? What is the spot market value of the material constituents? Ok, it's got cobalt, nickel, aluminum, carbon, some polymers for separation and a steel can.' So, break that down on a material basis and say: 'If we bought that on the London Metal Exchange, what would each of those things cost? Oh, jeez, it's like $80 per kilowatt-hour.' So, clearly you just need to think of clever ways to take those materials and combine them into the shape of a battery cell and you can have batteries that are much, much cheaper than anyone realizes."

In this example, there's a way in which Musk could've been even more precise and beginner friendly. Although he obviously thought about this, it's important to point out. Even more fundamental than "the material constituents of a battery" is the question, "What IS a battery?"

If you ask that question, you'll land on the answer: a battery is a device that stores energy for later. That's the most fundamental truth about a battery—because it's the definition. From there, we can think about what the battery is made of ("the material constituents"), and then we can think about how it's made. Those are slightly higher-level, but still very foundational truths. All of these truths are far closer to the ground than the idea that "battery packs are expensive." Assuming "battery packs will always be expensive" is essentially equivalent to spouting conventional wisdom— "It's always going to be the way it's always been."

When you start with foundational truths at that ground level, you can see and learn things that aren't obvious to those who accept conventional wisdom.

Musk's insistence on applying first-principles thinking to batteries has paid off. Tesla is leading the electric car revolution, and that wouldn't have been possible if they had adhered to conventional wisdom. Musk has been told he couldn't revolutionize many things: EV transportation, rockets, AI/human symbiosis, social media… Yet he's making more progress in these industries than practically anyone else in the world. How? By starting with first principles.

For the record, first-principles thinking isn't a new idea. Musk is just one great modern thinker in a long line of great thinkers throughout history who did their best to get down to bedrock. A few others who come to mind are Johannes Gutenberg, Henry Ford, René Descartes, Alexander Graham Bell, and Aristotle. They all pursued the fundamentals of reality ceaselessly, looking for the most basic principles that form the foundation of what we know and believe.

4. SCHOOL ≠ EDUCATION

PRINCIPLE:

DO NOT RELY ON SCHOOL
FOR YOUR EDUCATION.

Don't equate school with learning. School should be a place that accelerates and strengthens learning, but it often fails to do those things. You have the power to educate yourself, especially with the internet.

QUOTES:

> "There's no need to even have a college degree at all, or even high school... if somebody graduated from a great university, that may be an indication that they will be capable of great things but it's not necessarily the case."

"You don't need college to learn stuff. Everything is available, basically for free. You can learn anything you want for free; it is not a question of learning. There is a value that colleges have, which is seeing whether somebody can work hard at something, including a bunch of annoying homework assignments."

—

"I do agree with Peter [Thiel]'s point that a university education is often unnecessary. That's not to say it's unnecessary for all people. You probably learned the vast majority of what you're going to learn there in the first two years, and most of it is from your classmates. Because you can always buy the textbooks and just read them. No one is going to stop you from doing that... Now for a lot of companies, they do want to see the completion of the degree because they are looking for someone who's going to persevere and see it through to the end and that's actually what's important to them. So, it really depends on what somebody's goal is. If the goal is to start a company, I would say there's no point in finishing college. In my case, I had to, otherwise I would get kicked out of the country."

—

"What is the purpose of universities at this point? I think it's mostly just to hang out with peers, have some fun, and talk to your friends."

———

"You can learn whatever you need to to start a successful business either in school or out of school. School, in theory, should help accelerate that process; I think oftentimes it does [quote from 2003]. It can be an efficient learning process, perhaps more efficient than empirically learning lessons. But really, there are examples of successful entrepreneurs who never graduated high school, and then there are those that have PhDs. I think the important principle is to be dedicated to learning what you need to know whether that is in school or empirically."

———

"When you go through college... you have to answer the question that the professor gives you. You don't get to say, 'This is the wrong question.' In reality, you have all the degrees of freedom of reality, and so the first thing you should say is 'This question is wrong.'"

———

"I want to make sure Tesla recruiting does not have anything that says 'requires university' because that's absurd. But there is a requirement of evidence of exceptional ability. If you're trying to do something exceptional [work at Tesla], they must have evidence of exceptional ability. I don't consider going to college evidence of exceptional ability. In fact, ideally, you dropped out and did something."

—

"Don't be afraid of new arenas. You know, you can get a book and you can learn something and experiment with your hands and just make it happen. Find a way or make a way to get something done."

—

"I had to learn how to make hardware. I never had seen a CNC machine or laid out carbon fiber. I didn't know any of these things. But if you read books and talk to experts, you'll pick it up pretty quickly, but I think people self-limit their ability to learn. It's really pretty straightforward, just read books and talk to people—particularly books. The data rate of reading is much greater than when somebody is talking. What's the output rate of speech? It's like, a couple hundred bits per second, maybe a few thousand bits per second if you're really going full tilt. You can do several times that reading. The main reason I didn't go to lectures in college was because the data rate was too slow."

—

"Generally, you want education to be as close to a video game as possible... You do not need to tell your kid to play video games. They will play video games on autopilot all day. If you can make it interactive and engaging, then you can make education far more compelling."

—Elon Musk

APPLICATION:

Musk believes that to have an efficient, well-structured mind, you must avoid conventional schooling. His conviction regarding education was strong enough to take his kids out of an elite private school. Musk, along with one of the teachers from the private school, started a brand-new school called Ad Astra (since renamed Astra Nova). This school, as you might imagine, is unique. There are no grades. Musk doesn't believe in grades:

> "It shouldn't be that you've got these grades where people move in lockstep and everyone goes through English, math, science, and so forth from 5th grade to 6th grade to 7th grade like it's an assembly line. People are not objects on an assembly line. That's a ridiculous notion. People learn and are interested in different things at different paces. So, you really want to disconnect the whole grade level thing from the subjects. Allow people to progress at the fastest pace that they can or are interested in, in each subject. It seems like a really obvious thing."

But the fundamental principle that Musk instilled at the school was this:

"When you're trying to learn something, it's extremely important to establish relevance, to say: 'Why are you trying to learn this?' Because our minds are constantly trying to forget things. Our minds at a subconscious level, are trying to decide what is relevant and what is not relevant. So, most of the things you see and hear, your mind does not want to remember because there's no point in remembering it. So, you have to establish relevance... you want to say: 'This is why you should learn this subject or that subject' and once you establish relevance, your mind will naturally want to remember it. There are two fundamentally different ways to approach education: one is by teaching to the tools and the other is teaching to where you want to solve a problem and trying to understand what tools you need to solve the problem. So, for example, it would be quite boring to have a series of lectures about wrenches and screwdrivers and winches and whatnot, without establishing relevance. But if you say: 'Well, let's take apart an engine, now how do we take this engine apart and put it back together? Well, let's take apart an engine, now how do we take this engine apart and put it back together? Well, we're gonna need screwdrivers, we're going to need wrenches, we're going to need a winch, and we'll need maybe some Allen keys,' you'll take it apart and put it back together and then you'll understand in the process of doing that why those tools are relevant, and you'll remember them. This is a very simple but important principle, which is: explain the tools in the process of solving a problem, and then the tools will make sense, otherwise they will seem irrelevant, and people will not remember them and motivation will be difficult."

Musk continues in the same interview:

"You might take a course on calculus, for example, but you don't know why you're taking a course on calculus; it just seems like a mental obstacle course that doesn't have any point. And actually, for a lot of people I would say it probably is a mental obstacle course that has no point because unless you expect to use it in the future, there's no point in learning calculus—at least at a detailed level. I think the principles of calculus are interesting to learn but not the sort of nuanced solving of equations. So, I would generally say, like, what is it that somebody wants to do, and then try to solve that problem, and as you solve the problem say: 'Well, you need this tool, you need that tool...' Frankly, I think a lot of education that happens is kind of pointless, in that people are taught a bunch of things but they don't actually ever use those things in the future. So, why go to the trouble of teaching people things they will not use in the future... unless one simply wants to go through a mental obstacle course and test people's ability to go through a mental obstacle course... I think it's debatable as to whether we should force people to go through these mental obstacle courses. But if I could make a strong recommendation for what should be taught early in education[†] it is critical thinking. Critical thinking is incredibly important because it creates mental firewalls to allow children to reject concepts that are not cogent. It's sort of like having an anti-mind virus defense system. Critical thinking, if taught at a young age, creates a mental firewall that prevents false concepts from establishing themselves in people's minds. So, I would strongly recommend that the principles of critical thinking be taught at a young age."

Musk's school has been successful so far. Many more students besides Musk's kids have attended. The children attending the school loved the environment so much that they thought their vacations were too long... Big difference from an average student's attitude toward school.

---

† This book is organized in a manner to support Musk's ideas about education. We make each theoretical principle relevant with practical examples. Experience is the greatest teacher in life, so sharing Musk's experiences is incredibly important. As Musk discussed above, if you know why these principles would be helpful to you, you're much more likely to remember them and be able to use them when the time comes.

5. GET IT DONE, OR DIE TRYING

PRINCIPLE:

DO WHAT MUST BE DONE.

When adversity comes, persevere. Your "best" won't always cut it when your goal is ambitious, but you can do better. Don't give up irrationally, because if you continue to push and do what's required for the mission, you will surpass your "best" and expand far beyond what you ever thought was possible.

QUOTES:

> **Interviewer (Scott Pelley):** "When you had that third failure in a row, did you think: 'I need to pack this in?'" [rocket blew up]
>
> **Musk:** "Never. I don't ever give up. I mean, I'd have to be dead or completely incapacitated."

—

[Lex Fridman asks about where Musk gets his source of strength when challenges arise] "A source of strength, hmm...That's really not how I think about things... for me it's simply: this is something that is important to get done and we should just keep doing it or die trying. And I don't need a source of strength." Lex continues "So, quitting is not even like a..." and Musk finishes: "It's not in my nature. And I don't care about optimism or pessimism. Fuck that, we're gonna get it done."

—

"I think my drive to get it done is somewhat disconnected from hope, enthusiasm or anything else. I actually just don't care about hope, enthusiasm, motivation... I just give it everything I've got irrespective of what the circumstances may be... you just keep going and get it done."

—

"I certainly have lost many battles, so far I have not lost a war, but I have certainly lost many battles... more than I can count probably."

—

"We haven't gone into orbit yet, true, but we've made considerable progress. If it's an all-or-nothing proposition, then we've failed. But it's not all or nothing. We must get to orbit eventually, and we will. It might take us one, two or three more tries, but we will. We will make it work." [quote from Musk before SpaceX reached orbit]

—

"Persistence is extremely important. You should not give up unless you're forced to give up, you know, unless there's no other choice. Now that principle can be misapplied if you happen to be trying to penetrate a brick wall with your head... You have to be cautious in always saying one should always persist and never give up, because there actually are times when you should give up, because you're doing something in error. But if you're convinced that what you're doing is correct, then you should never give up."

—

"My proceeds from PayPal after tax were about $180 million; a hundred of that went into SpaceX, 70 into Tesla, and 10 into SolarCity. And then I literally had to borrow money for rent."

—

"If we don't succeed, then we will be certainly pointed to as a reason why people shouldn't even try for these things [space exploration]. So, I think it's important that we do whatever is necessary to keep going."

—

"Running companies hurts my heart, but I don't see any other way to bring technology and design to fruition."

—

"I don't think I want to delegate. I would love to delegate more. If people knew the full—I mean, probably if investors of Tesla knew the full scope of all the things that I do at Tesla, they would be quite concerned. Not because I want to, but it's just: 'OK, I need to get this done, I need to get this done. I can't find anyone to do it. I need to get it done, so I've got to do it.' It's not from some desire to keep things close to my vest. I would love to delegate more if at all possible. But the practical reality of it is that I cannot delegate because I can't find people to delegate it to."

—

Musk: "Tesla was under the most relentless short seller attack in the history of the stock market... Tesla was the most shorted stock in the history of stock markets... This was affecting our ability to hire people, it was affecting our ability to sell cars, it was terrible. They wanted Tesla to die so bad they could taste it."

Chris Anderson, TEDx: "Well, most of them have paid the price."

Musk: "Yes... Where are they now?"

———

"I'm available 24/7 to help solve issues [at Tesla]. Call me at 3 am on a Sunday morning, I don't care."

———

"For my part, I will never give up, and I mean never." [after the Falcon 1 blew up for the 3rd time in 2008]

———

"I will not let you down, no matter what it takes." [after taking over Twitter]

—Elon Musk

APPLICATION:

2008 was an excruciating period of Musk's life (and for many others as well). He had blown up three Falcon 1 rockets, Tesla was on the brink of bankruptcy, he was getting divorced, and the $180 million he had made from selling PayPal in 2002 was essentially gone (in fact, he was in debt, borrowing money from friends to pay rent). His appearance was horrendous. He was pale and skinny, and his eyes had sunken in. His then-wife Talulah Riley said: "He looked like death itself." The nights were the worst: "He would climb on me and start screaming while still asleep."

Pain.

Yet, Musk never let go. He willed his way through the horror. At the time of writing this, Musk is the wealthiest human being alive, and his companies are more successful than ever. In 2008 (and many times really), Musk pushed all his chips into the center of the table and did not back down, even against insurmountable odds. He did what needed to be done.

6. CAREERS AND PASSIONS

PRINCIPLE:

BUILD A CAREER AROUND A PASSION.
DON'T BUILD PASSION AROUND A CAREER.

The former will provide you with energy and fulfillment; the latter will starve you of both. Find a way to monetize what you love. When you're doing what you love (or what you feel you're called to do), you actually gain energy through your work.

QUOTES:

"If you like what you're doing, you think about it even when you're not working; it's something that your mind is drawn to and if you don't like it, you just really can't make it work, I think."

—

"People work better when they know what the goal is and why. It is important that people look forward to coming to work in the morning and enjoy working."

—

"There are three things you look for: You have to look forward in the morning to doing your work. You do want to have a significant financial reward. And you want to have a possible effect on the world. If you can find all three, you have something you can tell your children."

—

"You want to wake up in the morning and think the future is going to be great—and that's what being a spacefaring civilization is all about. It's about believing in the future and thinking that the future will be better than the past. And I can't think of anything more exciting than going out there and being among the stars."

—

Appreciate all the good wishes. First bday I've spent in the factory, but it's somehow the best." [2017 – when you're doing what you love, the need to escape on holidays diminishes]

—Elon Musk

APPLICATION:

Musk hasn't built any of his companies in pursuit of money alone. Every venture was unleashed in pursuit of something Musk cares about. He has been able to endure brutal circumstances running these companies because he loves his work. Do you think he would have been able to endure for decades if he had been working on things he wasn't passionate about? No. He's able to muster incredible energy daily because his work gives him energy. He is aligned with his calling and is energized as a result. Read this next quote:

> "There are a lot of negative things in the world, there's a lot of terrible things that are happening all over the world, all the time. There are lots of problems that need to get solved, they're miserable and kind of get you down. But life cannot just be about solving one miserable problem after another, that can't be the only thing. There needs to be things that inspire you, that make you glad to wake up in the morning and be part of humanity... There was a guy called Tsiolkovsky, one of the early Russian rocket scientists. He had a great saying: 'Earth is the cradle of humanity, but you cannot stay in the cradle forever.' It is time to go forth, become a star-faring civilization, be out there among the stars, expand the scope and scale of human consciousness... I find that incredibly exciting. That makes me glad to be alive. I hope you feel the same way."

Don't you get a deep sense of passion from that quote? Life is too short to pursue things that don't make you feel alive.

7. CONFORMITY = DEATH OF POTENTIAL

PRINCIPLE:

DO NOT SEEK CONFORMITY.

Avoid the herd. If you want to be all you can be, you must lean into your unique and innate abilities. Conforming may offer short-term comfort, but you'll suffer long-term pain due to a loss of potential.

QUOTES:

"I think people can choose to be not ordinary. You know, they can choose to not necessarily conform to the conventions that were taught to them by their parents."

—

"Most people in the corporate world really try to conform to some sort of behavioral thing that makes them seem like an android, drone, or some NPC in a video game with a limited dialogue tree."

—

"I thought, nobody is going to be crazy enough to do space, so I better do space."

—

"In the beginning, nobody wanted a Tesla, I can tell you that. We made the original Roadster sports car and people were like: 'Why would I want an electric car? My gasoline car works fine.' And I'm like: 'No, the electric car is better, you should try it.' It was hard to get people to do a test drive. First of all, nobody knew who we were… they'd never heard of this company… and I'm like: 'Yeah, we're named after Nikola Tesla. Do you know that guy?' [they responded] 'Nope.' So, for sure we were doing 'push' in the beginning because there was no one telling us they wanted an electric car. It was not like there were lots of people coming up to me saying: 'Hey, I really want an electric car.' I heard that zero times."

—

"Being a mom is just as important as any career." [for the women who want to dedicate their time to homemaking]

—

"I don't really compare myself to anyone. There are some people that I admire from history that I think are great. Certainly many of the scientists and engineers and literary figures and so forth. I'm a big fan of Ben Franklin; he was a scientist and thinker... He was the kind of guy that did what needed to be done. I wouldn't say I compare myself in any way, but I certainly admire them."

—

"Well, I think generally, I would recommend really communicating a lot on Twitter and I think it's good for people to speak in their voice as opposed to how they think they should speak. You know, like, sometimes people think: 'Well, I should speak in this way that is expected of me,' but it ends up sounding somewhat at times a bit stiff and not real. You know, if you read a press release from a corporation it just sounds like propaganda. So, I would encourage CEOs of companies and legislators and ministers and so forth to speak authentically... I think sometimes there's a concern about criticism, but I think at the end of the day, having some criticism is fine, it's really not that bad. I mean, I'm constantly attacked on Twitter, frankly, and I don't mind."

—

"Our stores are designed to be informative and interactive in a delightful way and are simply unlike the traditional dealership with several hundred cars in inventory that a commissioned salesperson is tasked with selling. Our technology is different, our car is different, and, as a result, our stores are intentionally different."

—Elon Musk

APPLICATION:

Musk has always done things his own way: building a car, building a rocket, and then launching the car into space on the rocket, drilling tunnels under cities, and posting hilarious memes that violate the standard CEO/businessman rulebook. The list goes on. Musk doesn't adhere to anyone's standards. He's never caved to the pressure to act 'normal'—even during his childhood in South Africa, when he was bullied relentlessly for being different.

Once, Musk and his brother were just sitting peacefully at the top of a flight of stairs and some bullies hunted him down:

"I was basically hiding from this gang that was fucking hunting me down for God knows fucking why. I think I accidentally bumped this guy at assembly that morning and he'd taken some huge offense at that."

One of the boys kicked Musk in the head and then pushed him down the flight of stairs. After he fell down the length of the stairs, the group rushed him and kicked him in the side, and the leader of the group bashed his head into the floor. He was beaten so badly that he blacked out, woke up in the hospital, and couldn't return to school for a week.

The bullying didn't end with physical harm. The bullies also demanded that Musk's friends stop hanging out with him. They did everything they could to torture the young man, both physically and emotionally.

> "There was a level of violence growing up that wouldn't be tolerated in any American school. It was like *Lord of the Flies*. There were a couple of gangs that were pretty evil, and they picked their victims, and I was one of them. I think part of what set them off was that I ended up sticking up for this one kid who they were relentless on. And that made me a target."

Eventually the bullying stopped thanks to a growth spurt. During those years, Musk developed a code for confrontation which he still stands by today: "I try not to pick fights, but I do finish them." Despite severe consequences, this unwillingness to change himself in his youth paid off well later. Once he landed in Silicon Valley, where his ambitions aligned with the environment and the people working there, he was well compensated for not conforming.

Now imagine what would've happened if Musk had reacted

differently. Imagine if he'd decided to give in to the social pressure, to believe what the bullies were telling him about his value, and to stop pursuing his strange passions and interests out of a desire to be accepted. Imagine if he had gone along with the "popular opinion" expressed by the bullies, or tried to blend in so that his friends were "allowed" to hang out with him. Would he have reached the heights he later attained?

I don't think he would have. Personally, I've seen several examples of young people who caved to criticism early on, gave up on their dreams, and ended up doing less than they might have done otherwise—because of the pressure to conform. It's a shame to see potential die in such a way.

8. EVOLUTION AND THE WORLD TODAY

PRINCIPLE:

STUDY HUMAN NATURE.

Understanding biology and evolution allows you to temper your impulses and commandeer your evolved strengths. We have millions of years of evolution ingrained in our minds and bodies. Most of your day-to-day actions are governed by this evolutionary force, so you want to be aware of what's going on. Awareness of human nature allows you to avoid the countless pitfalls that come from our "animal" selves and capitalize on the positive aspects.

QUOTES:

"We are all chimps. We're one notch above a chimp."

—

"Reasons to hate are remembered better than reasons to love. An evolutionary asymmetry helpful to survival, but counterproductive when survival is not at stake."

—

"The whole notion of being 'left wing' or 'right wing' is silly. Almost no one initially agrees with the semi-random collection of policies associated with each wing. They only support those policies *after* they join the left or right mind tribe."

—

"The Democrat vs Republican tribalism among otherwise intelligent people is most distressing. Demonizing everyone who would vote for an alternate party is not constructive."

—

"The limbic instinct for vengeance is incredibly strong, which is why turn the other cheek is such a powerful idea. As it ends the cycle of retribution."

—

"War always gives ample reason for vengeance for all sides. Only by overcoming this instinct can there be peace."

—Elon Musk

APPLICATION:

Musk is acutely aware of what's going on when it comes to evolution's impact in modern times:

> "Ultimately, we operate on two layers; we have sort of a limbic primitive layer, which is where all of our impulses are coming from. It's sort of like we got a monkey brain with a computer stuck on it—that's the human brain. And a lot of our impulses and everything are driven by the monkey brain and the computer, the cortex, is constantly trying to make the monkey brain happy. It's not the cortex that's steering the monkey brain, it's the monkey brain steering the cortex... The cortex is like what we'd call human intelligence, that's the advanced computer relative to other creatures. Other creatures do not have the computer, or they have a very weak computer relative to humans... [laughing] It seems like, surely the really smart thing should control the dumb thing, but actually, the dumb thing controls the smart thing... The difference between your cortex and your limbic system is gigantic. Your limbic system really has no comprehension of what the hell the cortex is doing. It's just literally: hungry or tired or angry or sexy or something, you know. The [limbic system] communicates that impulse and tells the cortex to go satisfy that [feeling]... A massive amount of thinking, like a truly stupendous amount of thinking has gone into sex—without purpose, without procreation... which is actually quite a silly action in the absence of

procreation. It's a bit silly, so why are you doing it? Because it makes the limbic system happy, that's why."

With this information, think over your life. Evolutionary drives are always pulling your strings, but you don't have to let that cause you trouble as a modern human being.

One of the products of evolution that Musk focuses on most is how we're still so vulnerable to tribalism—especially in politics. Musk has noticed this pattern, and he tries to engage the cortex or logical brain as much as possible. You can see it in how he tries to stay politically neutral and adhere to independent thinking:

"To be clear, I support the left half of the Republican Party and the right half of the Democratic Party."

"While it's true that I've been under unfair & misleading attacks for some time by leading Democrats, my motivation here is for centrist governance, which matches the interests of most Americans."

"To independent-minded voters: shared power curbs the worst excesses of both parties, therefore I recommend voting for a Republican Congress, given that the Presidency is Democratic."

"You know Twitter is being fair when extremists on far right and far left are simultaneously upset! Twitter aims to serve center 80% of people who wish to learn, laugh & engage in reasoned debate."

"Just a note to encourage people of different political or other views to engage in civil debate on Twitter. Worst case, the other side has a slightly better understanding of your views."

One of the big differences between Musk and [insert any

politician] is that he actively, visibly tries to avoid tribal rhetoric and agitation.

Are you aware of how your biology is affecting you? If so, are you actively making an effort to own your evolved strengths and temper unwanted impulses? The world would be a better place if everyone did that.

9. LEADING FROM THE FRONT

PRINCIPLE:

WORK ON THE FRONT LINES.

Leading from the front builds immense trust and boosts morale significantly. If you are building a company and your employees see that their leader is 100% committed and willing to do whatever it takes to succeed in the mission, they will work an order of magnitude harder. On the other hand, it's hard to fight for someone who has little skin in the game.

QUOTES:

"I lived in the Fremont and Nevada factories for three years fixing that [Tesla] production line, running around like a maniac through every part of that factory, living with the team. I slept on the floor so the team who was going through a hard time could see me on the floor and they knew that I was not in some ivory tower and whatever pain they experienced, I had it more."

—

"It's important for a leader to be at the frontlines. Our biggest challenge is ramping up production and so, what's that about? It's about being in the factory and understanding where the issues are. I want the very opposite of being up in an ivory tower, I want to be in the middle of the battle and so that means putting my desk in the middle of the factory. So, that's where it is [Musk points to his desk in the literal middle of the factory during a tour he gave]"

—

"I mean, my desk has frequently been in the factory. This is not some new thing. On the Model S ramp, my desk was also in the middle of the factory at the start of the body line for a year. So, I move my desk around to wherever the most important place is for the company. And then I sort of maintain a desk there over time to sort of come and check in on things."

—

"Spent the day walking entire Giga Berlin production line - team is doing excellent work!"

—

"Work ethic expectations would be extreme, but much less than I demand of myself." [on Twitter work environment]

—Elon Musk

APPLICATION:

There are lots of stories about Musk leading from the front. For example, when Musk and Tesla were dealing with the Model 3 production, it was as painful for Musk as the 2008 era:

"I was living in the factory in Fremont and the one in Nevada for 3 years straight, that was my primary residence. I'm not kidding. I slept on a couch, at one point in a tent on the roof and for a while there I was just sleeping under my desk which is out in the open, in the factory... and for an important reason: it was damn uncomfortable sleeping on that floor; when I woke up, I would smell like metal dust... there's a little conference room and a couch there, I stopped using the couch and just slept on the floor so during shift change the entire team could see me. This is important because if they think their leader is off somewhere having a good time, drinking Mai Tais on a tropical island, which I could definitely have been doing and would much have preferred to do... I'm not actually a masochist, I think... but since the team could see me sleeping on the floor during shift change, with nothing, they knew I was there, and that made a huge difference; they gave it their all."

Musk's willingness to get his hands dirty provides strong morale to his employees. Wars are largely won and lost on morale; the corporate world is no different.

Another excellent example of Musk serving on the frontlines was in the early days of SpaceX. The SpaceX team was trying to perfect a cooling chamber for its rocket engines. They had gone through a few chambers for $75,000 a pop while stress-testing them. After cracking all three, Musk took the hardware on his plane back to the Tesla factory in California for repairs. They got it on the factory floor and with the help of some engineers they began filling the chamber with epoxy to see if the chamber could be sealed. Mueller (one of SpaceX's top engineers at the time) described the scene: "He's out there with his nice Italian shoes and clothes and has epoxy all over him. They were there all night and tested it again and it broke anyway." Musk was a mess, but they got the hardware tested. They came to the conclusion the hardware had a flaw. Most leaders would never consider ruining their expensive clothes working with their employees—but Musk didn't care. He was there to get shit done, progress the mission, and lead.ϕ

ϕ Interesting history anecdote—leading from the front is a trait shared by numerous great leaders. Examples: Alexander the Great, Napoleon Bonaparte, Julius Caesar, Sun Tzu, etc. Alexander the Great would lead his men into battle and then afterward eat with and even apply medical aid to his wounded soldiers.

10. PROACTIVE VS. REACTIVE

PRINCIPLE:

LIVE PROACTIVELY.

Proactivity is anticipating problems and solving them when they're small—not waiting until they get big. There's a big difference between living proactively vs. reactively. Life is a lot less painful if you're in a proactive state.

QUOTES:

> "I think that we should be really concerned about AI. AI is a rare case where I think we need to be proactive in regulation instead of reactive because I think by the time we are reactive in AI regulation, it's too late."
>
> —

"I think as long as we continue to be worried and concerned and work hard towards sustainability, then we will achieve sustainability."

—

"There are time extensions on the game [using fossil fuels], but the game is going to come to an end. That should be absolutely certain—obviously, frankly… if you're in non-renewables, it's like you're stuck in a room where the oxygen is gradually depleting, and then outside, it's not. You want to get out of that room. The ones that get out of the room sooner will be better off."

—

"The question isn't 'Can you prove that we're making the planet warmer?' but 'Can you prove we're not?' And you can't. Think of that famous experiment about children and gratification. The kid who can delay his gratification for the cupcake for five minutes will be the more successful kid. That's us, but we're the unsuccessful kid. We will run out of oil and we're engaged in this dangerous experiment of pushing carbon dioxide into the atmosphere. It's crazy."

—

"I believe in the scientific method, and one should have a healthy skepticism of things in general, and from a scientific standpoint, you always look at things probabilistically, not definitively. A lot of times, if somebody is a skeptic in the science community, what they're really saying is that they're not sure that it's 100% certain that this is the case. But that's not the point. The point is to look at it from the other side and say: 'What do you think the percentage chance is of this [climate change] being catastrophic for some meaningful percentage of the Earth's population? Is it greater than 1%? If it is even 1%, why are we running this experiment?' We're playing Russian roulette [with the atmosphere] and, as each year goes by, loading more rounds in the chamber. It's not wise."

—

"I don't have any fundamental dislike of hydrocarbons. I simply look at the future and say, 'What is the thing that will actually work?' and using a non-renewable resource obviously will not work."

—

"I'm probably a little less alarmist than some: I think the danger is actually further off than is sometimes thought. But, at the same time, the solution is also very far off because the amount of electric vehicles needed to make a difference is hundreds of millions. And it takes a long time for an industry this big to change."

—

"If we don't have sustainable energy generation, there's no way that we can conserve our way to a good future. We have to fundamentally make sustainable energy available."

—

"If we wait, if we delay the change, the best case is simply delaying that inevitable transition to sustainable energy. This is the best case if we don't take action now… The only thing we can gain by slowing down the transition is just slowing it down. It doesn't make it not occur. It just slows it down. The worst case, however, is more displacement and destruction than all wars in history combined."

—

"The probable lifespan of human civilization is much greater if we are a multi-planet species as opposed to a single-planet species. If we are a single-planet species, then eventually there will be some extinction event, either from humans or some natural thing. Now is the first time in the history of Earth that the window has opened, where it's possible for us to extend life to another planet. It's been four and a half billion years—that's a long time. That window may be open for a long time, and hopefully it is, but it may also be open for a short time. So, I think the wise move is to make life multi-planetary while we can."

—

"Making life multi-planetary expands the scope & scale of consciousness. It also enables us to back up the biosphere, protecting all life as we know it from a calamity on Earth. Humanity is life's steward, as no other species can transport life to Mars. We can't let them down."

—

"It's important that we accelerate the transition to sustainable energy. That's why it matters whether electric cars happen sooner or later. We're really playing a crazy game here with the atmosphere and the oceans. We are taking vast amounts of carbon from deep underground and putting this in the atmosphere... This is crazy. We should not do this. It's very dangerous. So, we should accelerate the transition to sustainable energy. The bizarre thing is that obviously, we are going to run out of oil in the long term; there's only so much oil we can mine and burn. It's tautological, we must have sustainable energy transport and energy infrastructure in the long term, so we know that's the endpoint, we know that. So, why run this crazy experiment where we take trillions of tons of carbon from underground and put it in the atmosphere and oceans? This is an insane experiment. This is the dumbest experiment in human history."

—Elon Musk

APPLICATION:

One of the reasons why big problems (like climate change) sit there unsolved for decades is that individuals are too pre-occupied with getting their basic needs met—food, shelter, relationship stability, and so on. This is the stuff at the base of Maslow's hierarchy of needs. In practice, being proactive means getting your basic needs met first, so that you may pick your head up and think about the future more easily.

Musk isn't one to kick the can down the road. He has taken care of his basics to a degree that enables him to work toward things that are much larger than himself. This comes up when he describes his Zip2 days. The early days were brutal. They had leaky ceilings and thirdhand rugs. Musk was hyper-focused on getting the business up and running, paying the rent, and keeping the lights on. He couldn't focus on much else.

But now that he has built a strong foundation, he can address all sorts of things. He can focus on things that loom in the future. Those include the climate situation, humanity's eventual need to leave Earth, and the looming potential threat of artificial intelligence.

Tesla is a proactive move against climate change. SpaceX

is a proactive move against the extinguishing of the light of Consciousness due to Earth becoming inhospitable. Neuralink is a proactive move to protect humans from being outpaced by AI—their tagline is "if you can't beat 'em, join 'em."

If it hadn't been for Musk breathing life into the stagnant electric car industry, who knows where we would be today? We might have ended up with slightly better internal combustion engine cars with decent lane-keeping. Instead, countless car companies are now announcing their own electric vehicles. If it weren't for Tesla putting pressure on them, people would still be mourning the EV1 that GM recalled and demolished (literally, look it up!).

11. IMPORTANCE OF PASSING THE GREAT FILTERS

PRINCIPLE:

HELP HUMANITY PASS THE GREAT FILTERS.

For Civilization to continue and survive long-term, we must pass certain filters that would otherwise relegate us to eventual extinction. Make an effort in this life, no matter how small, to help humanity do so.

QUOTES:

"If we are able to make life self-sustaining on Mars, we will have passed one of the greatest filters. That then sets us up to become interstellar. Earth is

~4.5B years old, but life is still not multi-planetary, and it is extremely uncertain how much time is left to become so."

—

"This really might come down to: are we going to create a self-sustaining city on Mars before or after World War 3?"

—

"Well, the lens of history is a good way to filter more versus less important things. And as you zoom out further and further the really important stuff stays, and the less important stuff goes away. Now, let's say you zoom out really far and look at the entire history of earth or history of life itself. What are the most important elements in the history of life itself? Forget about parochial concerns of humanity. What would any species, any intelligent species say: 'Oh, those were really important items?' Well, there's obviously, single-celled [life], multicellular life, plants and animals, the animals you know, [sea creatures] going out of the ocean onto land, having mammals, consciousness, [and] this [is] part of maybe ten or so big ones on that list. And on that list, you also fit the extension of life to multiple planets for the first time. It will be at least as important as life going from the oceans to land and arguably more important because life could [move] gradually from the oceans to land, and if it got a little uncomfortable on the beach, you can hop back in the ocean. But [to] go extending life to another planet is a huge quantum leap. You have to go hundreds of millions of miles across an extremely hostile environment to a planet which is completely unlike anything you've evolved to live on. And that's just really an extremely difficult problem. In fact, I think it's an impossible problem without the advent of consciousness. So, consciousness is a necessary precursor for that."

—

"This is the first time in the four and a half billion-year history of Earth that it's been possible to extend life beyond Earth. Before this, it was not possible. How long will this window be open? It may be open for a long time, or may be open for a short time. I think it would be wise to assume that it is open for a short time, and let us secure the future of consciousness such that the light of consciousness is not extinguished. And we should try to do this as quickly as possible."

—

"Rage, rage against the dying of the light of consciousness."

—

"We can't be one of those lame one-planet civilizations!"

—

"I'm trying my hardest [to create a bright future for humanity]! Perhaps more people might consider loving humanity. Our collective light of consciousness is a tiny candle in a vast darkness. Please do not let it go out."

—

"If you look at the history of life itself, the big milestones, you could say, are the advent of single-celled life of course, the advent of multicellular life, development of a skeleton...You know, there's maybe 10 or 12 on that scale. And on that scale the extension of life to another planet would also fit."

—

"From a resource standpoint, I'm talking about less than 1% of Earth's resources should be dedicated to making life multi-planetary or making consciousness multi-planetary. I think it should be somewhere in between how much we spend on lipstick and how much we spend on healthcare."

—Elon Musk

APPLICATION:

Where are the aliens? It's a question that puzzles everyone. The most famous formulation of this question is the Fermi Paradox, introduced by Nobel Prize-winning Enrico Fermi in 1950 during a lunch conversation.

Fermi thought: Considering how many habitable planets there are out there, statistically, it seems almost impossible for us to be alone in the Universe. Additionally, given that our solar system is fairly young in comparison to the rest of the Universe (around 4.5 billion years old, compared to 13.8 billion), and due to the fact that interstellar travel might be fairly easy to achieve over a long enough time span, the aliens should have visited Earth by now. So, why haven't they?

One explanation is the Great Filter hypothesis, developed by Robin Hanson. The Great Filter simply says that intelligent lifeforms must jump through many advancement-of-life hoops in order to reach the heights of Consciousness and Civilization, including these:

- A planet must exist in a star's habitable zone.

- Life must somehow develop on that planet.

- Those organisms must then develop to reproduce.

- Simple cells (prokaryotes) must evolve into more complex cells (eukaryotes).

- Multicellular organisms must develop.

- Sexual reproduction, which greatly increases genetic diversity, must take place.

- Complex lifeforms then must create tools to alter their environment significantly.

- Those organisms must create advanced, sophisticated technology that enables space colonization. (We are basically here today)

- The advanced spacefaring species must eventually go on to colonize other worlds and star systems while somehow avoiding going extinct.

After reading through these, you can see that we have come a long way.

We seem to be incredibly rare, or at least our level of Consciousness is. As a result, we have a duty to pass the final filters. Passing these final filters guarantees the long-term survival of Consciousness.

Again, if we get wiped out, what happens if no other lifeforms make it past the filters? What happens if no other entities expand Consciousness to a degree that allows them to understand the true nature of the Universe? What if the only intelligent life in the Universe is found on Earth and we lose the opportunity to become a multi-planetary species? What happens if we lose the opportunity to safeguard this precious light of Consciousness? The stakes of this predicament we're currently in are not well appreciated. In fact, if we fail to keep the candle of Consciousness lit, it could be the greatest tragedy ever. This is about as serious as it gets.

So, we should do everything in our power to make sure this unbelievable opportunity is not squandered.

Elon Musk plans to use SpaceX to help humanity pass the Great Filters. SpaceX is working toward building a system in which rockets are fully and rapidly reusable, just like airplanes are today. Musk suspects that we're going to need one million people to create a self-sustaining city on Mars. The rocket that's going to get all the material and people to the red planet is called Starship. Starship is massive, towering 170 feet higher than its close cousin, the Falcon 9 rocket. (Starship's total height is 394 ft). SpaceX currently uses

Falcon 9 to send satellites into orbit and astronauts and supplies to the space station. Musk's fundamental vision for Starship is clear:

> "A fully and rapidly reusable rocket—which has never been done before—is the pivotal breakthrough needed to substantially reduce the cost of space access. While most rockets are designed to burn up on re-entry, SpaceX is building rockets that not only withstand re-entry, but also land safely on Earth to be refueled and fly again."

Starship will be able to transport 100 people and 100 tons of material. Musk plans to build a total of 1,000 starships and launch three of them a day during the window when Mars and Earth are closest. This window occurs every 26 months. The goal is to get 1,000,000 people to Mars by 2050 using this strategy. By getting a self-sustaining city on Mars built, we would pass a significant Great Filter.† Plus, it would be incredibly exciting. As Musk puts it: "Science fiction should not be fiction forever!" We must pass the Great Filters!

φ The filter after humanity becomes multi-planetary will be for us to become multi-stellar (expand into a different solar system). Now that's going to be an adventure!

12. THE NATURE OF THE MEDIA

PRINCIPLE:

THE MEDIA AND NEWS ARE NOT
WHAT THEY APPEAR TO BE.

It is essential that you understand that the media is focused on profit. Your attention drives their profit, and the most effective way to keep you on their app, webpage, or TV channel is to invoke strong emotions—usually anger. And to ensure their long-term security—and the security of their delusions—they want control of the Narrative, which adds another layer to everything.

QUOTES:

"It's a shrinking pie for most of the traditional media companies and [it's] made them more desperate to get clicks, to get attention. When they're in a sort of desperate state, they will then tend to really push headlines that get the most clicks, whether those headlines are accurate or not, so it's resulted in my view... I think most people would agree, in a less truthful, less accurate news. Because they've got to get a rise out of people, and I also think it's increased the negativity of the news because... I think we have an instinctual negative bias, which kind of makes sense in that... like it's more important to remember where was the lion or where was the tribe that wants to kill my tribe, than where is the bush with berries. One is a permanent negative outcome and the other is like: 'Well, I might go hungry.' Meaning that there is an evolved asymmetry in negative versus positive stuff. And also historically, negative stuff would have been quite proximate, like it would have been near; [it] represented a real danger to you as a person if you heard negative news.Because historically, like a few hundred years ago, we're not hearing about what negative things are happening on the other side of the world or on the other side of the country, we only care about negative things in our village, things that could actually have a bad effect on you. Whereas now, the news very often seems to attempt to answer the question: 'What is the worst thing that happened on Earth today?' And you wonder why you're sad after reading that..."

—

"The media is a click-seeking machine dressed up as a truth-seeking machine."

———

"World violence being super low is probably counter-intuitive to most people. That's because modern media is a misery microscope."

———

"Most news outlets attempt to answer the question: 'What are the worst things happening on Earth today?' It's a big planet! Obviously, some bad things are happening somewhere at any given time, but focusing relentlessly on those things does not give an accurate picture of reality."

———

"The news is sometimes created, but always curated. The latter is most pernicious. On any given day, there are thousands of potential stories. By picking which stories are written about and how prominently they're placed, a handful of publishers control much of the public narrative."

———

"All news sources are partially propaganda, some more than others."

———

"It used to be: 'Internet guy will fail at rockets/cars!' Now it is: 'Rockets/cars guy will fail at internet!' Literally from same media outlets haha." [on his Twitter acquisition]

—

"The amount of national and international news headlines dedicated to three Tesla fires that caused no injury is greater than all of the gasoline fires that occurred in the United States, which from mid-last year to today is about a quarter million gasoline car fires, which caused about 400 deaths, something like 1,200 serious injuries. Our three non-injurious fires got more national headlines than a quarter million deadly gasoline car fires. That's mad. What the heck is going on? A new technology should have a spotlight on it, but it shouldn't have a laser on it."

—

I've now been through so many hero-to-villain cycles I've lost count.

—

"As Twitter pursues the goal of elevating citizen journalism, media elite will try everything to stop that from happening."

—

"I do try my hardest to be good and sometimes I fear that untrue negative stories about me may cause others to excuse their bad behavior to their conscience, because they think I'm doing it too, but I'm not!"

———

"Is there a company that exists that has not lost talent on Earth anywhere? Well, of course not. There's attrition at every company. What matters is, what's the longevity of key executives and personnel at the company? Do they stay there a long time or is there a lot of turnover? Our turnover is less than the industry average, not higher. That's why the article was so ridiculous. They use the example of the Tesla general counsel where they said Tesla had, in the course of one year, three general counsels. That sounds like a lot except whenever an executive position changes in a year, you have two. So, all that means is that the guy in the middle didn't work out."

———

"The media reports with great fanfare my predictions that are late, but rarely those that come early."

———

"So hard to find out what's going on in the world without being bombarded with news that makes one sad and angry!"

—

"At some point, we should probably do advertising as art/communication/entertainment and to support high-quality media." [on potential Tesla advertising to combat the hit pieces]

—

"I've had a long career in multiple industries; if you list my sins, I sound like the worst person on Earth. But if you put those against the things I've done right, it makes much more sense." [on media's focus]

—

"I'm a big believer in citizen journalism and following individual journalists over publications!"

—Elon Musk

APPLICATION:

A great example of the media acting foolishly in pursuit of profit/control happened when Musk first took over Twitter. A couple of random guys sat outside Twitter's headquarters and started discussing how they'd been fired from Twitter. They had never worked there in the first place, and their reported names were "Rahul Ligma" and "Daniel Johnson." They both said some off-the-wall things to the press in interviews. Rahul claimed "Michelle Obama [as he held up her famous book] wouldn't have happened if Elon Musk owned Twitter." Johnson ended his interview with this statement: "If free speech is, ya know, Nazis saying that, ya know, transwomen shouldn't, ya know, use women's locker rooms, awesome, I guess, mission accomplished—we'll see. But listen, I gotta touch base with my husband and wife. I gotta get out of here, alright?"

The joke flew right over the reporters' heads, and CNBC reported it as if it had been legitimate. They were possessed with anger because they're currently losing their grasp on the Narrative thanks to Twitter. Plus, they were starving for any story that would help them trash Musk, because they knew it would attract clicks.

The media has written infamous Musk hit pieces since he first entered the world stage. More than ever, his name gets clicks, and the media conglomerate knows it. In April of 2022, Musk decided to try buying Twitter and the media lost their minds (as they still are, a year later). It's difficult to understand how Musk's intentions of buying Twitter can be warped by the media to such an extent. He said: "My strong intuitive sense is that having a public platform that is maximally trusted and broadly inclusive is extremely important to the future of civilization."

But they have pulled every insult out of their hat in an effort to hold onto their delusion, control, and oligopoly on the Narrative. They've played the far-right card, the evil billionaire card, and they've even somehow claimed that Musk threatens our right to free speech. We have reached new levels of hypocrisy this year—it's difficult to discern between satire and reality at times. It's sad to watch how desperate the media has become. They have no problem defacing Musk. Here's Musk's macro take on all this:

"The media has strong negative bias and are driven by clicks (they can't help it). Unfortunately, I generate lots of clicks. But these things move in cycles. When it starts boring readers to knock me down, they will build me up. This cycle has happened so many times…"

Fortunately, Musk has a strong base of supporters who combat this endless stream of negativity.

Funny enough, the propaganda promoted by the media hasn't done much to hinder Musk's progress. In fact, it appears to be helping him. There's an old saying about how there's no such thing as bad publicity, and this appears to be a perfect case of just that. At this point, the media's rubbish is like water off a duck's back for Musk: "I hope they keep cursing me on Twitter, as it increases advertising revenue!"

While Musk and Twitter are being trashed in the news, the app recently achieved its highest user count of all time. The app has grown by more than 15 million active users since the acquisition. By the time you read this, who knows what that number will be… Musk certainly has a lot of work to do in turning Twitter around, but the app has an unbelievably bright future. Musk has shared how Twitter could become a tremendous force for good and it may even be able to lower violence worldwide through its ability to become a digital town square where words are exchanged, rather than bullets. The bird is freed, and hopefully, it continues to ascend. Support independent journalists and Twitter if you'd like to see greater freedom in the world!

13. THE NATURE OF POLITICS

PRINCIPLE:

BE WARY OF POLITICS.

The incentives of politicians are not aligned with the well-being of the public. This misalignment results in a constant production of negativity and drama. Be wary of involving yourself in this dysfunctional system.

QUOTES:

"Politics is a sadness generator."

—

"Politics is war and truth is the first casualty."

—

"Government paid Twitter millions of dollars to censor info from the public."

———

"It would appear that the so-called 'fringe minority' is actually the government."

———

"At the end of the day, governments respond to popular pressure. If you tell politicians that your vote depends on them doing the right thing with climate change, that makes a difference. If they're having a fundraising event or a dinner party or whatever and at every fundraising event and every dinner party, somebody's asking them: 'Hey, what are you doing about the climate?' then they will take action. I think you have tremendous power. You have the power to make the change. We definitely can't beat the oil and gas industry on lobbyists. That would be a losing battle. Exxon makes more profit in a year than the value of the entire solar industry in the United States [in 2015]. If you take every solar company in the United States, it's less than Exxon's profit in one year. There's no way you can win on money. It's impossible."

———

"Behavior follows the incentives for political power."

—Elon Musk

APPLICATION:

Like the media, the incentives for politicians are not aligned with the well-being of the people. In reality, most politicians only care about your vote and they have no real intentions of creating significant or lasting change. A great example of how politicians are not aligned with the 'good' was when Tesla was not invited to a recent EV Summit in 2021. No one is even close to Tesla regarding the production of electric vehicles. Tesla was responsible for an impressive 69% of U.S. EV sales in 2021. Smaller EV automakers like Ford, GM, and Chrysler were praised for their efforts, though, and when White House press secretary Jen Psaki was asked about the situation, she said: "I'll let you come to your own conclusions."

Obviously, this decision was a consequence of the power that unions have over the current Democratic Party. If there was some rational and unbiased reason for failing to invite Tesla, wouldn't it have been pretty easy for them to explain that? No answer is always an answer.

Musk shared this thought about the Democratic Party: "The degree to which the unions control the Dems is insane. It's like watching a sock puppet 'talk', but the hand inside the sock is way too obvious!"

Most politicians are not concerned with doing the right thing; they focus on getting people's votes, and whoever gives them those votes (or power) will be favored. Simple, but not well understood. There's a lot going on behind the scenes when it comes to politics.

14. YOU ARE WRONG

PRINCIPLE:

ALWAYS TAKE THE POSITION THAT YOU
ARE, TO SOME DEGREE, WRONG.

If you are not to some degree wrong, that means you are 100% perfect in your analysis or conclusion. What are the chances that that's true? Quite low. So always approach endeavors from the standpoint of being open to being wrong, but move in the direction of being minimally wrong.

QUOTES:

"Our view of reality is always wrong, just a question of how wrong."

—

"Always take the position that you are, to some degree, wrong, and your goal is to be less wrong over time. One of the biggest mistakes people generally make, and I'm guilty of it too, is wishful thinking. You want something to be true, even if it isn't true, and so you ignore the real truth because of what you want to be true. This is a very difficult trap to avoid."

—

"People do not think critically enough. Critical thinking is a skill in short supply. People assume too many things to be true without sufficient basis in that belief."

—

"Do you have the right axioms, are they relevant, and are you making the right conclusions based on those axioms? That's the essence of critical thinking, and yet it is amazing how often people fail to do that. I think wishful thinking is innate in the human brain. You want things to be the way you wish them to be, and so you tend to filter information that you shouldn't filter. That's the most common flaw that I see."

—

"I think people should be nicer to each other and give more credit to others and don't assume that they're mean until you know they're actually mean. It's easy to demonize people; you're usually wrong about it. People are nicer than you think."

—Elon Musk

APPLICATION:

Musk notices when he's been wrong in the past and takes steps to be aware of that in the future. For example, he learned that business plans are really just wishful thinking. In an interview with Musk, Jonathan Nolan asks:

"How do you plan a business where you know, the rocket business, you know some of these things are going to blow up on the launch pad? How does the business plan work?"

Musk responds:

"I didn't really have a business plan... [laughs]. I had a business plan way back in the Zip2 days, but these things are just always wrong, so I just didn't bother with business plans after that... Wishful thinking for sure is a source of many problems in many walks of life. Business or personal, wishful thinking causes a lot of trouble. You really have to ascertain whether something is true or not, does it make sense, and if it ever feels like it's too easy, it probably is."

You might not be launching rockets, but this principle applies to you no less than it does to Musk.

15. GIVE YOUR FOLLOWERS A NORTH STAR

PRINCIPLE:

> PAINT A MEANINGFUL PICTURE
> OTHERS CAN STRIVE TOWARD.

When in a leadership position, you must have a goal, BUT it must also be meaningful/unique. The problem is that most forget about the second part. There are a lot of stars in the sky, and if your star (goal) can't be differentiated from the others, you'll be adrift in the ocean of life.

QUOTES:

> "People work better when they know what the goal is and why. It is important that people look forward to coming to work in the morning and enjoy working."

—

"You first have to say, 'What is the goal?' And once you have 'What is the goal,' you can then measure various designs against that goal. Otherwise, you're saying 'Why is one design better than another?' What's your goal? There's got to be a goal. So, the goal is: get enough tonnage to Mars and enough people to make Mars self-sustaining as quickly as possible."

—

"Our goal when we created Tesla a decade ago was the same as it is today: to accelerate the advent of sustainable transport by bringing compelling mass-market electric cars to market as soon as possible."

—

"The goal of SpaceX is to revolutionize space travel. The long-term goal is to establish Mars as a self-sustaining civilization as well as to just kind of have a more exciting future."

—

"Right now, trajectory of neuro-silicon symbiosis doesn't appear to intersect trajectory of AGI. Goal of Neurlink is to raise this probability above 0.0%"

—

"Starlink's purpose is to provide internet to the least served and to pay for Mars."

—

"Our [The Boring Company's] goal is to solve traffic, which plagues every major city on Earth."

—

"The larger goal is to do the things that serve the greater interest of civilization and have Twitter ultimately be a force that is moving civilization in a positive direction, where people think it is a good thing for the world and the evidence for that will be new users signing up and more people using Twitter for longer. And then I think also, if you were to use Twitter for an hour a day, that when you look back, you don't regret the time… you don't want something that, say, is hyper-addictive, but you look back and you're like: 'Man, I kind of regret how I spent that hour.' You want to enjoy using Twitter and find it entertaining, informative, funny and then when you look back at the time you spent on Twitter, not regret it. Then I think we will have succeeded."

—

"Well, it's just a very small percentage of mental energy that is on the big picture. You know where you're generally heading for, and the actual path is going to be some sort of zig-zaggy thing in that direction. You try not to deviate too far from the path that you wanna be on, but you're going to have to do that to some degree."

—Elon Musk

APPLICATION:

Every one of Musk's companies has a clear, compelling, and differentiated goal. Neuralink's North Star is to achieve symbiosis with AI in an attempt to protect humanity, The Boring Company's North Star is to get rid of soul-destroying traffic, Tesla's North Star is to accelerate the advent of sustainable energy, SpaceX's North Star is to help humanity become a multi-planetary species, and Twitter's North Star is to establish the most trusted free-speech platform on the planet.

For many, Musk's most fascinating North Star is our emergence as a multi-planetary species thanks to SpaceX. This is also what moves Musk most deeply. He has stated that he is accumulating resources primarily to make the greatest contribution he can to enable multi-planetary life. Even though any one of his goals could easily be another's wildest dream, Mars tops them all.

In an excellent interview on the Joe Rogan Experience podcast, Rogan asks Garrett Riesman (who worked at SpaceX):

"Now, what is the timeline in terms of, like, does SpaceX have a multiple-stage timeline for incorporating the Dragon crew and then a timeline for the Star Hopper and then a timeline for additional projects in the future? Is he [Musk] thinking along the lines of, like, charted-out progress?"

Riesman responds: "Oh yeah, yeah. In fact, he measures

pretty much every major decision by whether or not it brings the day when we have a self-sustaining colony on Mars, sooner or later... every single decision he makes, he makes it through that prism."

Riesman confirms that Musk is hyper-focused on the grand goal and distributes this vision to everyone working at the company. Everyone knows full well that they're all at SpaceX to get humanity to Mars. Their results thus far reflect that focus and concrete vision. This exciting and meaningful mission gives employees a "why" that gets them through any "how." Through extreme stress, long hours, and insanely difficult problems, SpaceX employees have managed to push on with Mars as their North Star (or, perhaps, "North Planet"). Do you think people would endure all of the pain associated with building rockets if they were working at a laundromat? Maybe, depending on the leader... but probably not. The difference comes from the distinct and compelling North Star of making humanity a space-faring species!

16. THE NECESSITY OF HUMOR

PRINCIPLE:

HAVE A LAUGH.

Partake in humor. If you refuse to, you will not only make yourself miserable, but you'll bring down others as well. Look, no one really knows what's going on. Think about it. We're a bunch of advanced animals who are launching rockets into space, video chatting with each other on opposite sides of the world, splitting atoms… and we don't even know why we're here! It's wild! Yes, you should absolutely take this gift of life seriously and give it all you have, but it's necessary to take a step back every once in a while. Life is pretty absurd, so don't forget to have a laugh and relieve tension within yourself.

QUOTES:

> "My closest friends got a compilation of rocket failures and made me watch the whole thing… There were lots of people who tried to talk me out of it…

and the joke was: "How do you make a small fortune in the rocket business? Well, you start with a large one."

—

"I'd like to die on Mars, just not on impact."

—

"I actually met [at an event] a woman I dated briefly in college, who now works at Scientific American as a writer, and she related the anecdote that we went on a date and all I was talking about was electric cars... that was not a winning conversation... She said the first question I asked her was 'Do you ever think about electric cars?' [laughs] No, she never does! It wasn't great... but recently [after creating Tesla] it's been more effective [laughs again]."

—

"Don't want to brag but... I'm the best at humility."

—

"The rumor that I'm building a spaceship to get back to my home planet Mars is totally untrue."

—

"It [Tesla vehicle] seemed ludicrously fast. And I like *Spaceballs* as a movie. So, we named it 'Ludicrous Mode' for that reason. I mean, I thought it was funny—maybe not everyone thinks it's funny, but

I thought it was funny. I mean, it's memorable. I think people are going to remember 'Ludicrous Speed' more than they're going to remember that it's like 2.8 seconds 0 to 60. And our competitors, they usually don't have a sense of humor, so I think that's a differentiator."

—

"I think it would be fun to do a cover of 'Barbie Girl' but… 'Cyber Girl.' I'm a cyber girl, in a cyber world, it's fantastic, in the future there's no plastic."

—

"Unsure if confirming or denying that I'm an alien is more convincing that I'm an alien."

—

"I have Sam Gamgee's words on my bedside table." [funny but honorable at the same time]

—

"Trash me all day, but it'll cost $8."

—

"It would be kind of weird if the aliens landed in the ocean with parachutes… 'OK, nothing to fear…haha'" [on the absurdity of humans utilizing parachutes for space travel and why we need to be able to land rockets]

"In the past, victory would mean that your enemies are no longer around. These days, they're not only alive and well, but have lots of time on their hands to edit Wikipedia!"

—

"I hate sarcasm so much you can't believe it."

—

"One of my favorite conspiracy theories is that the world is actually 80% men."

—

"A friend asked me at a party, 'Hey, what are you going to call the third-generation car?' Well, we got the Model S and X, we might as well make it the E, you know. And then it kind of stuck, even though we were just kidding. And then just to sort of add to it, we also just for laughs trademarked the Model Y. But I guess things are pretty dry in the trademark world… nobody picked up on that. Then Ford gave us a call and said they were gonna sue us for using Model E… Ford's killing sex!"

—

"Please buy my perfume [Burnt Hair], so I can buy Twitter."

—

"I'm dressing up as a sink and knocking on random doors. Once they see me, they will have no choice but to let that sink in."

—

"Humor is one of the great joys of life!"

—Elon Musk

APPLICATION:

Musk claims his side hustle is comedy. The main outlet of this side hustle is his Twitter account. He often shares funny memes and they're often well-received. Most memes get hundreds of thousands of likes on the low end and one of his jokes: "Next I'm buying Coca-Cola to put the cocaine back in" got 4.7 million likes. 4.7 million likes on the notoriously stingy-with-engagement Twitter is insane. That tweet is the most liked Tweet by any living human… In a recent podcast, Musk explained his efforts regarding humor: "I strive to keep the people entertained. I wanna earn my keep in with the people." It's not a coincidence that Musk has the most interacted-with Twitter account in the world and he's a fan of comedy. Everyone loves comedy.

Musk's sense of humor isn't limited to Twitter. His companies are also an outlet for his comedic side hustle. The Boring Company tops them all when it comes to humor. Not only is the name witty (boring holes in the ground… which is dull), but they have hilarious products. The Boring Company sold a flamethrower and most recently, Burnt Hair Perfume. Here's Musk's rationale for creating the flamethrower:

> "We didn't put a lot of time into the flamethrower. This was an off-the-cuff thing. I have sort of a hobby company called The Boring Company which started out as a joke, and we decided to make it real and dig a tunnel under LA. Then other people asked us to dig tunnels and so, we said yes in a few cases. And then we have a merchandise section that only has one piece of merchandise at a time. We started off with a cap… and then, I am a big fan of *Spaceballs* the movie and in *Spaceballs*, Yogurt goes through the merchandising section, and they have a flamethrower in the merchandising section… 'The kids love that one,' that's the line [in the movie] when he pulls out the flamethrower. 'We should do a flamethrower.'" [Musk and his team actually did it]

Every bizarre product Musk has launched has sold out instantly. Humor allows you to connect and relate with people. Relatability and connection with others are huge when you're a leader.

17. WORK

PRINCIPLE:

PUT IN THE WORK.

In order to get incredible outputs (results) in life, you must put in equally incredible inputs (work). This is a Universal Law. It's just math. Every single successful individual has taken advantage of compounding by simply putting in more time and energy than most.

QUOTES:

"Work like hell. I mean, you just have to put in, you know, 80-hour, 80–100-hour weeks, every week... If other people are putting in 40-hour workweeks and you're putting in 100-hour workweeks, then even if you're doing the same thing… you will achieve in 4 months what it takes them a year to achieve."

———

"You're not going to create revolutionary cars or rockets on 40 hours a week. It just won't work. Colonizing Mars isn't going to happen on 40 hours a week."

———

"You have to apply a lot of hours to actually working. So, the way that I generally do it is: I'll be working at SpaceX on Monday, and then Monday night fly to the Bay Area. Then Tuesday and Wednesday at the Bay Area at Tesla, and then fly back on Wednesday night, spend Thursday and Friday at SpaceX. In the last several months, then I'd fly back here [Bay Area] on a Saturday and either spend Saturday and Sunday at Tesla or spend Saturday at Tesla and Sunday at SpaceX."

———

"When my brother and I were starting our first company, instead of getting an apartment we just rented a small office, and we slept on the couch. We showered at the YMCA, and we were so hard up that we had just one computer, so the website was up during the day, and I was coding at night. Seven days a week, all the time. And I sort of briefly had a girlfriend in that period and in order to be with me, she would have to sleep in the office."

———

"Work hard—like every waking hour. That's the thing I would say, particularly if you're starting a company."

———

"There's an old saying, it's like 1% inspiration and 99% perspiration, I think it might actually be 99.9% perspiration…"

—Elon Musk

APPLICATION:

Almost every time people ask Musk how he has accomplished all he has, he responds in a similar manner:

"I do put in a lot of hours. I'm not sure I would necessarily recommend what I do to others, in the sense that I pretty much work all the time. It's quite rare for me to take even a Sunday off."

Usually, he also mentions critical thinking, first principles, and physics as tools that amplify the effectiveness of the hours he puts in. At the time of this writing, Musk is building Twitter and has been putting in 16–17-hour days, 7 days a week, while sleeping at Twitter's headquarters. This may sound like a lot, but what's even more impressive is that he has been doing this for decades. Even back in the early Zip2 days, he could be found working around the clock and sleeping under his desk with a physics book as a pillow. The mental picture of Musk using a physics book as a pillow, while sleeping under his desk, sums up his persona perfectly. How many people do you know who would put that amount of time and dedication into their work? Exactly. Very few, if any. This is one of the primary reasons he has achieved what others haven't achieved. He has simply given time and energy that others haven't given.

18. DO COOL THINGS

PRINCIPLE:

JUST DO COOL STUFF.

Life is too short to not do cool stuff. Pretty simple.

QUOTES:

"Rockets are cool."

—

"Down the road, I'd love to work on something which is a vertical takeoff and landing supersonic electric jet, and leverage what I've learned from SpaceX and from Tesla to try to make that happen."

—

"Cybertruck will be waterproof enough to serve briefly as a boat, so it can cross rivers, lakes & even seas that aren't too choppy."

—

"SpaceX has more active satellites in orbit than rest of Earth combined, tracking to double rest of Earth soon." [2022]

—

"The party where I ended up wrestling with the world champion sumo wrestler, by the way, which also caused me to burst a disk in my neck. Five minutes of glory for five years of pain… that really hurt. That party was Victorian Japanese Steampunk, so that was cool."

—

"Why did we name one booster Falcon and one Dragon? Falcon is named after the Millennium Falcon from *Star Wars* because Falcon can do the Kessel Run in 7 parsecs. And then Dragon was actually named after Puff, the Magic Dragon because so many people thought I must be smoking weed to do this venture."

—

"When I was young, I didn't really know what I was going to do when I got older… Eventually, I thought that the idea of inventing things would be really cool and the reason I thought that was because I read a quote from Arthur C. Clarke, which said that 'A sufficiently advanced technology is indistinguishable from magic.' And that's really true. If you go back say 300 years, the things that we take for granted today, you'd be burned at the stake for... being able to fly... that's crazy, being able to see over long distances, being able to communicate, having effectively with the internet a group mind of sorts, and having access to all the world's information instantly from almost anywhere on the Earth... This is stuff that really would be considered magic in times past. In fact, I think it actually goes beyond that because there are many things that we take for granted today that weren't even imagined in times past, that weren't even in the realm of magic. So, it actually goes beyond that. So, I thought, well, if I can do some of those things, basically if I can advance technology then that's like magic and that'd be really cool."

———

"The internal name for designing the machine that makes the machine is the Alien Dreadnought. At the point at which the factory looks like an alien dreadnought, then you know you've won."

———

"I think a Tesla is the most fun thing you could possibly buy ever. That's what it's meant to be... It's not exactly a car. It's actually a thing to maximize enjoyment."

—

"I could not be more proud of everyone at SpaceX and all of our suppliers who worked incredibly hard to develop, test, and fly the first commercial human spaceflight system in history to be certified by NASA. It's a great honor that inspires confidence in our endeavor to return to the Moon, travel to Mars, and ultimately help humanity become multi-planetary."

—

"I ran out onto the causeway to watch the landing, and the sonic boom reached me about the same time as the rocket touched down, so I actually thought, at first, that it had exploded. But it turned out to be just that the sonic boom almost exactly coincided with the touchdown point, and the sound reached me several seconds later. I thought: 'Well, at least we got close,' but then I went back into launch control, and it was this amazing video of the rocket still actually standing there on the launchpad, or the landing pad, I should say. I can't quite believe it." [first time landing a booster]

—

"I think this is quite significant. I can't say exactly where it would rank, but I do think it's a revolutionary moment. No one has ever brought an orbital-class booster back intact."

—

"That was freaking awesome. We made orbit thanks to the hard work of the SpaceX team and all you guys—I mean, that's really what got us to orbit there. There were a lot of people who thought we couldn't do it—a lot, actually—but as the saying goes, fourth time's the charm. This really means a lot to SpaceX, obviously, getting to orbit—is just a huge milestone. There's only a handful of countries on Earth that have done it. It's normally a country thing, not a company thing. So, it's just an amazing achievement."

—

"I've never felt anything like [Tesla's acceleration speed]... It's faster than falling... It's like having your own roller coaster on tap."

—

"When the car is operating at maximum capability... We can't even detect any viruses or bacteria or spores. It's like zero comes through. So, if there's ever an apocalyptic scenario of some kind, hypothetically, you just press the Bioweapon Defense

Mode button—this is a real button. We're trying to be a leader in apocalyptic defense scenarios." [half-jokingly]

—

"We've actually spent a lot of effort on the space suit design—on both the functionality and the aesthetics. It's actually really hard because if you just optimize for functionality, it's one thing; if you optimize for aesthetics, it doesn't work. Those things that you see in movies, they don't work. So, it's like, how do we make something that looks cool and works? With the key goal here being that when people see the space suit, we want them to think: 'Yeah, I want to wear that thing one day.'"

—

"Initially I thought, well, perhaps it's a question of funding and that funding can be garnered by marshaling public support. So, I thought one way to get the public excited about space would be to do a privately funded robotic mission to Mars. So, we figured out a mission that would cost about $15-20 million, which isn't a lot of money but it's about a tenth of what a low-cost NASA mission would be. The idea was called 'Mars Oasis,' where we would put a small robotic lander on the surface of Mars with seeds and dehydrated nutrient gel, which would hydrate upon landing and you'd have plants growing in a Martian radiation and gravity conditions, and you'd also be maintaining essentially a life support system on the surface of Mars. And this would be interesting to the public because they tend to respond to precedents and superlatives, and this would be the furthest that life's ever traveled and the first life on Mars, so pretty significant."

———

"What was unique about the Roadster was it was the first really great electric car. And before the Roadster, people thought an electric car would be slow and ugly and low range and have bad performance. And we had to break that mold. It was incredibly important to show that that wasn't true."

———

"It was rated by almost every group as the best car in its year and by Consumer Reports as the best car ever. The reason for that is not just to achieve some superlative in cars but to show what an electric car can do—because nobody believed that an electric car could do this." [on the Model S]

———

If you go back a few hundred years, what we take for granted today would seem like magic—being able to talk to people over long distances, to transmit images, flying, accessing vast amounts of data like an oracle... So, engineering is for all intents and purposes, magic and who wouldn't want to be a magician?

———

"I'm not really a businessman… I'm sure there's probably lots of analysts on Wall Street that would agree that I am not a businessman… I'm an engineer… [I am a] technologist. I make new technologies, great new technologies. Technology is like magic. I think technology is the closest thing to magic that we have in the real world and so creative engineering is essentially technology development. And when I was a kid, *Lord of the Rings* was my favorite book and I thought: 'What's the closest thing to being a wizard in the real world?' And that's creating new technologies."

—

"If you think about the future, you want a future that is better than the past. So, if we had something like the Hyperloop, that would be like, 'Cool!' You'd look forward to the day that that was working. Even if it was only in one place, from L.A. to San Francisco or New York to D.C. or something like that. It would be cool enough that it would be like a tourist attraction, like a ride or something. So, even if some of the initial assumptions didn't work out and the economics didn't work out quite as one expected, it would be like, cool enough [to say] 'I want to journey to that place just to ride on that thing.' That would be pretty cool. If you come up with a new technology, it should feel like that."

—

"We will publish stats on Love Speech too [on Twitter], as it is vastly higher than Hate Speech!"

———

Jay Leno: "Is that a special kind of glass? Is that different from normal windshield glass?" [referring to Cybertruck glass]

Musk: "We are going to be using, effectively, a form of armored glass for the car, and the door panels of the car are 300 series stainless steel, and it's so tough that it's bulletproof to a handgun."

Jay Leno: "And why is it important to you that it be bulletproof?"

Musk: "Because it's badass... and super cool."

— Elon Musk

APPLICATION:

What's cooler than building a rocket-launching facility called Starbase, which will launch a vehicle called Starship, which has been built with the intention of colonizing another planet and making humanity a space-faring species? I mean c'mon...

Musk is working on and thinking about many cool things, but high on that list is terraforming Mars. It's obviously going to take a long time to terraform Mars into an Earth-like planet, but nonetheless, it's worth adding in here. Mars has a tremendous amount of ice on its surface, and the first step to terraforming the barren planet will be to melt that ice. Here is one of Musk's ideas for doing that:

> "Well, you could use solar reflectors, or you could just create artificial suns with a series of thermonuclear explosions. The sun is a giant thermonuclear reactor... If you launched a missile every 10 seconds and then [explosions and heat are produced]. It's like fireworks but real big... thermonuclear fireworks [laughs]. But you couldn't have a sustained reaction because the sun is a gravitationally contained thermonuclear reactor, so you need a lot of gravity. The sun is well over 99% of all the mass of the solar system. It's very big."

This future of terraforming Mars is an important part of SpaceX's Mars Mission. There is a massive poster in the SpaceX factory that depicts the stages of terraforming Mars. It is very cool and often ends up being Musk's Twitter banner as well. In the image, you can see the planet gradually transition from red and barren to blue and green—from death to life. Think about a terraformed Mars—new countries, "exotic" places. You could visit the massive mountain called Olympus Mons... just endless coolness to be experienced on a terraformed Mars.

19. ON UTILITY

PRINCIPLE:

STRIVE TO LIVE A USEFUL LIFE.

Try to be as useful as you can possibly be. And make sure you take the step of putting yourself in a position to be useful. Many overlook that part.

QUOTES:

> "That's generally my advice to people, try to be useful. It's very difficult to be useful to others. To do a genuinely useful thing to others, that's what we should all be trying to do. And it's very difficult…"

> —

"Whatever this thing is that you're trying to create, what would be the utility delta compared to the current state-of-the-art, times how many people it would affect? That's why I think having something that makes a big difference but affects a small to moderate number of people is great, as is something that makes even a small difference but affects a vast number of people."

—

"Well, I think there's just a certain amount of time and within that time, you want the best net outcome. So, for all the set of outcomes that you can do, there's going to be some which will fail, some which will succeed, and you want the net useful output of your set of actions to be the highest. So, like, you can use a baseball analogy; you know in baseball, they don't let you just sit there and wait for the perfect pitch until you get a real easy one. They're going to give you three shots and then after the third one, they say 'OK, get off the [mound], go back to the [dugout]… put somebody else up there…' So, what you're really looking for is like, what's your batting average? There's going to be some amount of failure, but you want your net output, your net useful output to be maximized."

—

"We have a lot of good people at SpaceX, a lot of really talented people. In fact, I wonder sometimes how we can make use of their talents in the best way because, you know, I think we're often not using their talents in the best way."

—

"It is better to approach this [building a company] from the standpoint of saying—rather than you want to be an entrepreneur or you want to make money—what are some useful things that you can do that you wish existed in the world?"

—

"Working hard to make useful products and services for your fellow humans is deeply morally good."

—

"My father was an engineer… If that hadn't been the situation, then I would have had little exposure to it, even in South Africa. Engineers should have more kids—whether it's nature or nurture, they [the kids of engineers] are more likely to become engineers. I'm doing my civic duty. I gotta make up for the lost ground of some others."

—

"I certainly hope they will work very hard. I believe they should be productive contributors to society. They shouldn't be trust-fund kids. I'm hopeful they will do things like engineering, or write books, or just, in some way, add more than they take from the world." [on his hopes for his children]

—

"I think, if somebody is doing something that is useful to the rest of society, I think that's a good thing. Like, it doesn't have to change the world, you know. If you're doing something that has high value to people and frankly, even if it's something like just a little game or some improvement in photo sharing or something, if it does a small amount of good for a large number of people… I think that's fine. Stuff doesn't need to change the world just to be good."

—

"I don't think everyone needs to go try to solve some big world-changing problem. I really think we should just think, 'Are we doing something useful to the world?' If you're doing something useful, that's great… Like, sort of a 'usefulness optimization' is a really good thing. If you've done something that's useful to your fellow human beings, you've done a really good thing, and people should feel proud of doing that. It doesn't always have to be something that's going to change the world, I mean sometimes the world should just keep going in a particular direction."

—

"I think what matters is the actions, not what people think of me in the future. I'll be long dead. But the actions that I take, will they have been useful?"

—Elon Musk

APPLICATION:

Musk's entire life is a testament to providing utility to others, so in this application, we'll focus on how to optimize yourself for utility. Musk has made an effort to optimize himself in various ways. Some of this self-optimization includes looking after his health for example. Musk is a fan of fasting: "On advice of a good friend, I've been fasting periodically and feel healthier." Not only has fasting proven to be beneficial scientifically, but it also makes sense from an evolutionary perspective. Throughout human evolution, our ancestors "practiced" fasting between meals. As a result, our internal system is set up for fasting to this day. When it comes to evolution, the longer something is done and the more often it is done throughout an organism's history, the more ingrained it will be in the biological system. This hearkens back to our earlier point about evolution. Considering the prehistoric eating schedule we maintained for thousands of generations, it's no surprise that many people feel healthier by replicating that pattern today.

Another essential aspect of self-optimization is proper relaxation or decompression. There are many ways to relax; you need to find the one that works for you. Musk said: "Some people use meditation or yoga to calm their mind at the end of the day, but video games on hardcore mode work best for me." Musk's mind is bombarded all day long with problems, and time spent playing video games allows him to switch off for a bit, or at least change the channel. So, if you struggle with relaxing and you've had little success with meditation or yoga, it could be time to try video games on hardcore mode!

In conclusion, the more you keep your body, mind, and soul well-maintained, the more useful you can be to yourself and others. Take care of yourself† to take care of others.

---

† One more quote from Musk that may be useful to you: "For improved quality of sleep, raise head of your bed by about 3in or 5cm, and don't eat 3 hours before bedtime." This quote is referring to how you may go about better optimizing your sleep. You'll never be able to be useful to others if you're tired all the time.

20. BUREAUCRACY IS BAD

PRINCIPLE:

TEMPER BUREAUCRACY.

As your organization grows, avoid the overdevelopment of bureaucracy. The layers of hierarchy that form in bureaucracies hinder innovation, communication and the efficiency of work in general. You need structure, but don't let things solidify too much.

QUOTES:

> "For a company, when it's very small, productivity grows quickly because of specialization of labor. Then productivity per person declines due to communication issues as a company gets bigger. As you have more and more layers through which

communication has to flow, that necessarily imparts errors. Every time information flows from one person to another, to another—even with the best of intentions—you have information loss... To the degree that you can alleviate that by doing things like skip-level meetings, I think it's a good idea."

—

"Excessive meetings are the blight of big companies and almost always get worse over time. Please get [rid] of all large meetings, unless you're certain they're providing value to the whole audience, in which case keep them very short."

—

"Also get rid of frequent meetings, unless you are dealing with an extremely urgent matter. Meeting frequency should drop rapidly once the urgent matter is resolved."

—

"Walk out of a meeting or drop off a call as soon as it is obvious you aren't adding value. It is not rude to leave, it is rude to make someone stay and waste their time."

—

"Don't use acronyms or nonsense words for objects, software or processes at Tesla. In general, anything that requires an explanation inhibits communication. We don't want people to have to memorize a glossary just to function at Tesla."

———

"Communication should travel via the shortest path necessary to get the job done, not through the 'chain of command.' Any manager who attempts to enforce chain of command communication will soon find themselves working elsewhere."

———

"A major source of issues is poor communication between depts. The way to solve this is to allow free flow of information between all levels. If, in order to get something done between departments, an individual contributor has to talk to their manager, who talks to a director, who talks to a VP, who talks to another VP, who talks to a director, who talks to a manager, who talks to someone doing the actual work, then super dumb things will happen. It must be OK for people to talk directly and just make the right thing happen."

———

"In general, always pick common sense as your guide. If following a 'company rule' is obviously ridiculous in a particular situation, such that it would make for a great Dilbert cartoon, then the rule should change."

—

"We really try to minimize the number of offices we have, because doors limit communication. Everyone at the company, with the exception of a few people in HR and finance, actually are in cubes, including vice presidents…"

—

"Everyone eats same food, uses same restrooms [at his companies], etc.—no executive chef or other ivory tower stuff. There shouldn't be this workers vs management two-class system. Everyone is a worker."

—

"I don't believe in process. In fact, when I interview a potential employee and he or she says that 'It's all about the process,' I see that as a bad sign. The problem is that at a lot of big companies, process becomes a substitute for thinking. You're encouraged to behave like a little gear in a complex machine. Frankly, it allows you to keep people who aren't that smart, who aren't that creative."

"Are CEOs in corporate America focused enough on product improvement? I think the answer is 'No.' And generally, my recommendation is to spend less time on finance, spend less time in conference rooms, less time on PowerPoint, and more time just trying to make your product as amazing as possible."

—

"I do so wish that more companies would put down their spreadsheets for a moment and focus on making products that move your heart."

—

"Most big companies in tech have turned into places where talent goes to die."

—

"I don't think the government intends to stand in the way of innovation, but sometimes it can over-regulate industries to the point where innovation becomes very difficult. The auto industry used to be a great hotbed of innovation at the beginning of the twentieth century, but now there are so many regulations... The body of regulations for cars could fill this room, it's crazy how much regulation there is, like down to what the headlamps are supposed to be like, they even specify some of the elements of the user interface on the dashboard and some of these are completely anachronistic."

—

"Rules and regulations are immortal. And if we keep making more every year, and do not do something about removing them, then eventually we'll be able to do nothing."

—

"I'm generally a fan of minimal government interference in the economy. The government should be the referee but not the player, and there shouldn't be too many referees. But there is an exception, which is when there is an unpriced externality, such as the CO_2 capacity of the oceans and atmosphere. When you have an unpriced externality, then the normal market mechanisms do not work, and then it's government's role to intervene in a way that's sensible. The best way to intervene is to assign a proper price to whatever the common good is that is being consumed."

—

"Tragically, it is not clear that the defense contractors can get to the Moon for any amount of money. More than $200B has been spent on development of new US crewed space transport systems over past ~40 years, but only Dragon is flying. Development cost to NASA was <$2B."

—

"One [problem] is the incredible aversion to risk within big aerospace firms. Even if better technology is available, they're still using legacy components, often ones that were developed in the 1960s... Everyone is trying to optimize their ass-covering."

—

"We built this incredible technology [at Zip2], but it wasn't being used by the customers in the right way. It's a bit like building F-22 fighter jets and then you sell them to people, and they roll them down the hill at each other... If you got great technology, you want to go all the way to the end consumer. Don't sell it to some bonehead legacy company that doesn't understand how to use it."

—

"A weird thing happens when companies get big: most companies or organizations, the bigger they get, they tend to get less innovative. Not just less innovative on a per-person basis but less innovative in the absolute, and I think this is probably because the incentive structure is not there for innovation.

It's not enough to use words to encourage innovation; the incentive structure must be aligned with that, that's fundamental."

—Elon Musk

APPLICATION:

Back in 2020, right before SpaceX sent astronauts to the space station, Musk wanted to optimize the chances of this mission's success. He did whatever it took to make that happen:

"Cargo can be replaced, crew cannot. So, the level of scrutiny, the level of attention, is an order of magnitude greater... it was already high for cargo but it's just a whole nother level for crew. I told the SpaceX team that this mission reliability is not merely the top priority, it is the only priority right now. So, we're just doing continuous ensuring reviews from now, nonstop, 24 hours a day, until launch, just going over everything again and again and again. I was out at the pad just recently walking down the rocket—we've got a team that's just crawling over the rocket in the horizontal, then we're gonna rotate it vertical, then we're gonna crawl all over it in the vertical. We're just looking for any possible action that can improve the probability of success no matter how small, whether that comes from an intern or me or anyone, doesn't matter."

This isn't how most companies operate. Most organizations

move slowly, inhibited by countless barriers to communication, endless chains of command, and a bureaucratic sign-off culture that prevents anyone from taking initiative. They're too weighed down by paperwork to launch something great.

21. SCALING TECHNOLOGY

PRINCIPLE:

UNDERSTAND THE NATURE OF SCALING TECHNOLOGY

Each new technological development follows the same pattern. A new technology is initially only available to a small minority of people—at a relatively high price. As innovation continues and scale rises, the price of the technology drops, and more people adopt it. Also, scaling is hard.

QUOTES:

"If you think of, say, phones...the earliest cell phones, like in the original [movie] *Wall Street*, the guy's walking down the beach and he's [carrying] a giant phone... and all it could do was phone. And it had 30 minutes of battery life. At that time, in the absence of technology improvements, no amount of money, no amount of scale could have made that phone affordable. There had to be a lot of engineering iterations, a lot of design iterations. And we're probably, I don't know, on the 30th version of a cell phone and with each successive design iteration, you can add more capability, you can integrate more things, you can figure out better ways to produce it. So, it actually gets better and cheaper. It's a natural progression of any new technology—it takes multiple versions and a large volume in order to make it affordable."

—

"If we could have done that [produce a mass-market electric car] with our first product, we would have, but that was simply impossible to achieve for a startup company that had never built a car and that had one technology iteration and no economies of scale. Our first product was going to be expensive no matter what it looked like, so we decided to build a sports car, as that seemed like it had the best chance of being competitive with its gasoline alternatives."

—

"We've realized that the true problem, the true difficulty, and where the greatest potential is, is building the machine that makes the machine, in other words, building the factory. And really thinking of the factory like a product... We don't try to create a car by ordering a bunch of things off a catalog. We design the car the way it should be and then we, or working with suppliers, make all of those individual components. There's almost nothing in a Model S that's in any other car. And I think the same approach is the right approach to take when building the machine maker, the factory. I actually think that the potential for improvement in the machine that makes the machine is a factor of 10 greater than the potential on the car side. I think maybe more than a factor of ten."

—

"This is something that the average person really has no idea about whatsoever. Not just the average person. Smart people on Wall Street have, usually, not the faintest clue about manufacturing and how difficult it is. They think that once you have come up with a prototype, well, that's the hard part. And everything else is trivial copying after that. It is not. That is perhaps 1% of the problem. Large-scale manufacturing, especially of a new technology, is somewhere between 1,000% and 10,000% harder than the prototype. I would really regard, at this point, prototypes as a trivial joke."

—

"The extreme difficulty of scaling production of new technology is not well understood. It's 1,000% to 10,000% harder than making a few prototypes. The machine that makes the machine is vastly harder than the machine itself."

—

"You can create a demo version of a product, like a few cars worth of a product, with a small team in maybe three to six months. But to build the machine that builds the machine, it takes at least a hundred to a thousand times more resources and difficulty."

—

"Prototypes are easy, production is hard."

—

"Many times, we've been asked, 'If you reduce the cost, don't you reduce reliability?' This is completely ridiculous. A Ferrari is a very expensive car. It is not reliable. But I would bet you 1,000-to-1 that if you bought a Honda Civic that that sucker will not break down in the first year of operation. You can have a cheap car that's reliable, and the same applies to rockets."

—

"I came to the conclusion that there wasn't really a good reason for rockets to be so expensive and they could be a lot less. Even in an expendable format, they could be less, and if one could make them reusable, like airplanes, then the cost of rocketry will drop dramatically, the cost of space travel would drop dramatically."

—

"At this point, I think designing a rocket is trivial, just trivial. There's like, tons of books—you read 'em and if you can understand equations, you can design a rocket. Real easy... Now making even one of those things and getting it to orbit is hard."

—

"People who don't create products and services don't realize that it takes hard work to produce products and services."

—

"If you're going to create a company the first thing you should try to do is to create a working prototype. Everything looks great on PowerPoint. You can make anything work on PowerPoint but if you have an actual demonstration article, even if it's in primitive form, that's much, much more effective for convincing people."

—Elon Musk

APPLICATION:

In this example, we are going to explore Tesla's original master plan. Here's an excerpt from The Secret Tesla Master Plan (just between you and me) written by Elon Musk in 2006:

"Background: My day job is running a space transportation company called SpaceX, but on the side, I am the chairman of Tesla Motors and help formulate the business and product strategy with Martin and the rest of the team. I have also been Tesla Motor's primary funding source from when the company was just three people and a business plan.

"As you know, the initial product of Tesla Motors is a high-performance electric sports car called the Tesla Roadster. However, some readers may not be aware of the fact that our long-term plan is to build a wide range of models, including affordably priced family cars. This is because the overarching purpose of Tesla Motors (and the reason I am funding the company) is to help expedite the move from a mine-and-burn hydrocarbon economy towards a solar electric economy, which I believe to be the primary, but not exclusive, sustainable solution.

"Critical to making that happen is an electric car without compromises, which is why the Tesla Roadster is designed to beat a gasoline sports car like a Porsche or Ferrari in a head-to-head showdown. Then, over and above that fact, it has twice the energy efficiency of a Prius. Even so, some may question whether this actually does any good for the world. Are we really in need of another high-performance sports car? Will it actually make a difference to global carbon emissions?

"Well, the answers are no and not much. However, that misses the point, unless you understand the secret master plan alluded to above. Almost any new technology initially has high unit cost before it can be optimized, and this is no less true for electric cars. The strategy of Tesla is to enter at the high end of the market, where customers are prepared to pay a premium, and then drive down market as fast as possible to higher unit volume and lower prices with each successive model.

"Without giving away too much, I can say that the second model will be a sporty four-door family car at roughly half the $89k price point of the Tesla Roadster and the third model will be even more affordable. In keeping with a fast-growing technology company, all free cash flow is plowed back into R&D to drive down the costs and bring the follow-on products to market as fast as possible. When someone buys the Tesla Roadster sports car, they are actually helping pay for development of the low-cost family car."

At the end of the plan, Musk summarizes everything:

"Build sports car.

Use that money to build an affordable car.

Use that money to build an even more affordable car.

While doing above, also provide zero emission electric power generation options.

Don't tell anyone."

Awesome to see how far Tesla has come!

This piece of writing is useful because it sheds light on how new technology progresses and scales. When a technology is first introduced, it is expensive and available to only a small minority of people. Phones, computers, and gas cars were once only available to a tiny, wealthy minority. But as innovation continued, manufacturers developed better processes, and the increase in production capacity slowly dropped the price. Now all of those things are pretty cheap. This is the process that every technology goes through. Understanding this progression for any new technology is helpful when it comes to fully comprehending the nature of innovation and technology at large. Many talk about how a certain piece of tech is "too expensive" and no one will ever be able to afford it, but all you have to do is look back through history and you can see the reality of the situation. Keep this in mind if you're looking to bring a new technology to market.

22. MERITOCRACY RULES

PRINCIPLE:

STRUCTURE YOUR ORGANIZATION WITH MERITOCRACY.

When building your company or organization, put competence first. If people are put into positions of power for any other reason (like ass-kissing or diversity...), you'll have a sub-optimal organization. The more competence and experience you have in a particular dimension, the more responsibility you should be granted.

QUOTES:

"I strongly believe that all managers in a technical area must be technically excellent. Managers in software must write great software or it's like being a cavalry captain who can't ride a horse!"

"I think, just generally the path to leadership should not be through an MBA business school situation. It should be, kind of, work your way up and do useful things… There's a bit too much of the 'somebody goes to a high-profile MBA school and parachutes in as the leader,' but they don't actually know how things work. They could be good at PowerPoint presentations or something like that and they can present well, but they don't actually know how things work because they parachuted in instead of working their way up…They're not aware of what's really needed to make great products. I don't wanna trash MBAs too much here and I actually do have a dual undergrad, a Wharton undergrad and physics at UPenn. So, I have direct exposure to business school… but I think it's just a little bit too much like people look at MBA school as: 'I want to parachute into being the boss, instead of earning it.' And I think that is not good."

—

"I'd much rather promote someone who has strong engineering ability than so-called management ability. We do hire some MBAs, but it's usually in spite of the MBA, not because of it."

—

"If you look at, say, the Tesla Autopilot AI team, it's about 150 engineers, and they're outperforming teams that they're competing against that are 3,000 engineers. I'm a big believer that a small number of exceptional people can be highly motivated and can do better than a large number of people who are pretty good and moderately motivated. That's my philosophy. And those who go hardcore and play to win, Twitter is a good place. And those who are not, totally understand. But then Twitter is not for you."

—

"Anyone who can be in office, should be. However, if not logistically possible or they have essential personal matters, then staying home is fine. Working remotely is also ok if their manager vouches for excellence." [on working from home policy]

—

"Executive competence is super underrated in politics - we should care about that a lot more!"

—

"I wish politicians were better at science, that would help a lot."

—

"I'm head engineer and chief designer, as well as CEO [at SpaceX], so I don't have to cater to some money guy. I've encountered CEOs who don't know the details of their technology and that's ridiculous to me."

"It's pretty nerve-racking, that's for sure. The pucker factor on launch date is very high. It should be said, I'm actually a physics guy, I'm an engineer really and do the business stuff because you kind of have to do the business stuff, or if you don't do the business stuff, someone else is going to do it for you and then you could be in trouble… I'm actually the chief designer of the rocket. I could redraw that rocket without the benefit of blueprints for the most part, so it's sort of like seeing my baby go up there."

—

"At this point, I think I know more about manufacturing than anyone currently alive on Earth. I can tell you how every damn part in that car is made."

—

"Capital allocation should be done by those best at doing so."

—

"I really just look for evidence of exceptional ability, or at least aspiration. Sometimes these things get messed up in recruiting, or the recruiting filter ends up being wrong. I sometimes wonder, with Tesla, if Nikola Tesla applied to Tesla, would we even give him an interview? It's not clear. You know, 'This guy came from some weird college somewhere in Eastern Europe, he's got some odd mannerisms, we don't know if we should give him an interview'—I worry that that's actually what we do instead. It should be like, 'Man, Nikola Tesla, this kid's super smart. What does he want? We'll pay him anything!'"

—

"We should actively recruit the best and brightest to be part of the United States! That is what every championship sports team does."

—Elon Musk

APPLICATION:

Musk is a proponent of meritocracy.[φ] Tesla and SpaceX are high on the list of desirable places to work, and Musk tries to ensure they stay high on that list because he wants to attract the highest-quality people. The missions of Musk's companies demand extreme competence. Musk makes this explicit when he talks about building teams:

"I want to accentuate the philosophy that I have with companies in the startup phase, which is a sort of 'Special Forces' approach. The minimum passing grade is excellent. That's the way I believe startup companies need to be if they're ultimately going to be large and

---

φ Maybe one day there will be an official Musk University that is governed by meritocracy. It would be the most efficient university in the world...

successful companies. We'd adhered to that to some degree, but we strayed from that path in a few places. That doesn't mean the people that we let go on that basis would be considered bad—it's just a difference between Special Forces and regular Army. If you're going to get through a really tough environment and ultimately grow the company to something significant, you have to have a very high level of dedication and talent throughout the organization."

Competent people get shit done. Tesla and SpaceX get shit done. That's a pretty simple puzzle to piece together.

23. RATE OF FIXING MISTAKES

PRINCIPLE:

FIX MISTAKES AT THE QUICKEST
RATE YOU CAN MANAGE.

You are going to make mistakes no matter the endeavor; the difference lies in how quickly you fix your mistakes. Some people never correct their mistakes and give up after facing them. Some correct their mistakes, but it takes them a long time to do it. And some accept their mistakes in stride while correcting them as quickly as possible. The people in each of these groups all live very different lives.

QUOTES:

"The success of a company is very much more about how quick are you to fix the mistakes, not will you make mistakes."

—

"If you see the difference between a startup that is successful and one that is not, it's because they both made mistakes but the successful one recognized the mistakes, fixed them very quickly, and the unsuccessful one tries to deny that the mistakes exist."

—

"We have a philosophy of continuous improvement. Every week, there are approximately 20 engineering changes made to the car... Other manufacturers tend to bundle everything together in a model year. In our case, it's a series of rolling changes, so [the] model year doesn't mean as much."

—Elon Musk

APPLICATION:

I'm hesitant to include this example because it's unclear how Twitter may fare in the coming years, but it's just too good not to include.

One of the more exciting examples of Musk putting this principle into action is with the recent Twitter acquisition. He's making bold moves, failing, and fixing those mistakes quickly with Twitter 2.0. Within a couple of weeks, Musk began implementing significant changes. Most CEOs would take a month to familiarize themselves with the company, hear people out, and take things slow—not Musk though. After only a few weeks of running Twitter, he implemented a new verification system. This implementation had some bugs, so they paused it, reworked things, and relaunched the updated verification system. This is one of many rapid developments we have seen take place at the company.

Musk knows from his past experiences running his other companies that they're guaranteed to fail to some degree, but what's important is that they keep moving:

> "The key is to be extremely agile, and so if we do make a dumb move, or when we make a dumb move, because we're not going to always knock the ball out of the park, but when we make a dumb move, we correct it quickly—that's what really matters."

The company that is least afraid of failure and the most willing to fix its mistakes, and rapidly, will run laps around everyone else. The same goes for individuals.

Who knows how this Twitter experiment will turn out, but so far, the results speak for themselves. Since the purchase, free speech is now allowed again. There's more engagement on the app than ever, they're releasing all the nonsense shadow work that happened in the past, and they've done more to prevent child exploitation in one month than the company had previously done in 10 years. Every day, Twitter is becoming an even more excellent place to spend time. There are problems, but that's just part of the ride. Both Tesla and SpaceX struggled in the beginning. Twitter is no different, but it's headed in a positive direction. Make sure to contribute in whatever way you can to the growth of Twitter—this may just mean tweeting!

24. DOING THE RIGHT THING

PRINCIPLE:

JUST DO THE RIGHT THING.

Do what you know deep down is right. It may hurt in the short term, but it will pay off in the long term.

QUOTES:

"Honestly, I really am just trying to do the most amount of good with the time that I have on this Earth. And, you know, not always succeeding, but that's the goal."

—

"I am a strong believer in doing the reality of good over the perception of good… So, we're just gonna take the heat… If we know we're gonna get sued [at Tesla] despite doing the right thing, we will do the right thing and get sued."

—

"We always try to do the right thing [at Tesla]. We really care about that. When we make mistakes, it's just because we were being foolish or stupid or whatever, but it's really always made with the right motivation."

—

"I think it's worth investing your own capital in what you do. I don't believe in the sort of the 'other people's money thing.' I think, if you're not willing to put your own assets at stake, then you shouldn't ask other people to do that."

—

"You wanna get up in the morning and be excited about the future. We should fight for the things that make us excited about the future. The future cannot just be about one miserable thing after another, solving one problem after another. There has got to be things that get you excited like you want to live… I'm trying my hardest to do so [work towards a bright future]. I love humanity and we should fight for a good future for humanity. I think we should be optimistic about the future and fight to make that optimistic future happen."

—

"The whole point of Tesla is to accelerate the advent of electric vehicles and sustainable transport. We're trying to help the environment; we think it's the most serious problem that humanity faces. I'm not sure if you [the interviewer] knew, but we open-sourced our patents so anyone who wants to use our patents can use them for free… If somebody comes and makes a better electric car than Tesla and it's so much better than ours that we can't sell our cars and we go bankrupt, I still think that's a good thing for the world."

—

"Tesla Motors was created to accelerate the advent of sustainable transport. If we clear a path to the creation of compelling electric vehicles, but then lay intellectual property landmines behind us to inhibit others, we are acting in a manner contrary to that goal. Tesla will not initiate patent lawsuits against anyone who, in good faith, wants to use our technology."

—

"The overarching goal of Tesla is to accelerate the advent of sustainable energy and so if we created a patent portfolio that discouraged other companies from making electric cars, that would be inconsistent with our mission. So, we open-sourced all the patents in order to help anyone else who wants to make an electric car."

—

"I should add a note here to explain why Tesla is deploying partial autonomy now, rather than waiting until some point in the future. The most important reason is that, when used correctly, it is already significantly safer than a person driving by themselves, and it would therefore be morally reprehensible to delay release simply for fear of bad press or some mercantile calculation of legal liability."

—

"We think it actually is going to make a difference to the world if we transition to sustainable transport sooner rather than later. We're not doing this because we thought it was a way to get rich."

—

"Tesla will argue for autonomous driving, but we're not going to argue against manual driving. And I believe people should have the freedom to choose to do what they want to do. And, yes, sometimes those things are dangerous, but freedom is important. If people want to drive, even if it's dangerous, they should be allowed to drive in my view. But then the autonomous safety systems should be in there such that even if you're in manual mode, the car will still aid you in avoiding an accident."

—

"We've already opened Tesla Superchargers to other electric cars in Europe and we intend to roll that out worldwide. It's a little trickier in the US because we have a different connector than the rest of the industry. But we will be adding the rest of industry connectors as an option to Superchargers in the US. We're trying as best as possible to do the right thing for the advancement of electrification—even if that diminishes our competitive advantage."

—

"I have made it a principle within Tesla that we should never attempt to make servicing a profit center. It does not seem right to me that companies try to make a profit off customers when their product breaks. Overcharging people for unneeded servicing (often not even fixing the original problem) is rampant within the industry and happened to me personally on several occasions when I drove gasoline cars. I resolved that we would endeavor never to do such a thing at Tesla."

—

"In designing the Model S and the Model X, safety was our absolute paramount goal. I felt like, obviously, my family will be in the car, my friends' families—if I didn't do everything possible to maximize safety and something went wrong, I couldn't live with myself."

—

"Creating a new car company is extremely difficult and fraught with risk, but we will never be a company that by our action does, or by our inaction allows, the wrong thing to happen just to save money."

—

"What Tesla's motivation is, is to make electric transport as affordable as possible. That is what informs all of our actions. So, if we do something, and we charge for this or charge for that, it is not because we want to make things more expensive, it's because we can't figure out how to make it less expensive, that's all."

—

"The more I learn [about Twitter's secret history], the worse it gets. The world should know the truth of what has been happening at Twitter. Transparency will earn the trust of the people."

"I'm fine with Trump not tweeting. The important thing is that Twitter correct a grave mistake in banning his account, despite no violation of the law or terms of service. Deplatforming a sitting President undermined public trust in Twitter for half of America."

—

"Removing child exploitation [on Twitter] is priority #1. Please reply in comments if you see anything that Twitter needs to address."

—

"It has been really bad [Twitter motives]. Far left San Francisco/Berkeley views have been propagated to the world via Twitter. I'm sure this comes as no surprise to anyone watching closely. Twitter is moving rapidly to establish an even playing field. No more thumb on the scale!"

—

"Twitter will not censor accurate information about anything."

—

"Anyone suspended for minor and dubious reasons will be freed from Twitter jail."

—

"Twitter should be as broadly inclusive as possible, serving as a fair forum for lively, even if occasionally rancorous, debate between widely divergent beliefs."

—

"Someone has to have a phone and a credit card and $8 a month. That's the bar. However, we will actively suspend accounts engaged in deception or trickery, of any kind. So, it is a leveling of the playing field. It will be less special to have a checkmark, but I think this is a good thing… I think it's going to be a good world. I mean… don't we believe in one person, one vote? I think we do… I actually just don't like the lords and peasants situation where some people have blue check marks, and some don't. You know, at least in the United States we fought a war to get rid of that stuff… this is just philosophically how I feel and maybe this is a dumb decision, but we'll see." [on new Twitter verification for all idea]

—

"Twitter's current lords and peasants system for who has or doesn't have a blue checkmark is bullshit. Power to the people! Blue for $8/month."

—

"I have not been trying to optimize on a risk-adjusted return basis. I would not say that I went into the rocket business or the car business or the solar business thinking that it's a great opportunity. I just thought that something needed to be done in these industries in order to make a difference and that's why I did it."

—

"We believe in doing deals where both parties benefit and when there is an asymmetry or under performance on our part, interpreting that in the other party's favor... Our goal in doing so is to build long-term trust. If people know that we will not take advantage of them and aspire to fairness, even at our own expense, then they are much more likely to want to work with us in the future."

—

"I think part of the reason people aren't as excited about space is that we haven't been pushing the frontier as much. You can only watch the same movie so many times before it gets a little boring. In the 60s and early 70s we were really pushing the frontier of human spaceflight. Landing on the moon is regarded as one of the greatest achievements of humanity, arguably of life itself. And even though only a handful of people went to the moon, vicariously we all went there. Well, at least I wasn't alive at the time, so, retrospectively [laughs]... It was just one of those really inspiring things that made everyone glad to be human. There's bad things humanity does and good things, and this is one of the good things. I do think it's important that we have these inspiring things that make you glad to get up in the morning and glad to be a member of the human race. We need to push that frontier. The great goal we should be trying to pursue is to make life multi-planetary, to establish a self-sustaining and growing civilization on another planet, Mars being the only realistic possibility. I think that would just be one of the greatest things humanity could ever try to do."

—

"It will be increasingly difficult to see Starlink satellites, as we're actively working with the astronomer community to ensure that even the most sensitive telescopes are fine and scientific progress is not impeded."

—

"I've been up all night trying to think of any possible way to de-escalate this war." [Ukraine 2022]

—

"I care a lot about the truth of things and trying to understand the truth of things."

—Elon Musk

APPLICATION:

Musk's strong moral compass made an appearance in April of 2022. Musk and SpaceX announced that they would be supporting Ukraine by providing internet to war-torn regions through their Starlink satellite internet system. Only a small percentage of the service has been paid for, and it has cost SpaceX $20 million a month to operate and maintain. This isn't an ideal situation, as Musk's goal for the new service was to simply "not go bankrupt."

Currently, the US Department of Defense is refusing to aid SpaceX in providing internet access to Ukraine. This is madness considering the money they've sent over already. Additionally, Starlink is the one and only line of communication that can be used reliably. Musk tweeted: "Internet fiber, phone lines, cell towers and other spaced-based comms in war areas have been destroyed."

SpaceX has also had to divert its efforts toward defending against jamming attacks and other modes of cyber warfare. When Musk was rejected by the US Department of Defense, he sent this tweet out: "The hell with it… even though Starlink is still losing money & other companies are getting billions of taxpayer $, we'll just keep funding Ukraine govt for free."

This situation really boggles the mind. If they were in Musk's position, most people would have great difficulty holding the fort and staying true to their beliefs. Yet, Musk continues to do what he believes is right, despite the unbelievable circumstances.

One of the best ways to guard against immoral behavior is

to abandon a zero-sum mindset. In an interview, Lex Fridman asked Musk about his advice for young people. Musk said:

> "Generally, to not have a zero-sum mindset… or have more of a grow-the-pie mindset, if you sort of say like, when you see people perhaps… including some really smart people… doing things that seem morally questionable, it's often because they have at a base axiomatic level, a zero-sum mindset without realizing it. They don't realize they have a zero-sum mindset or at least they don't realize it consciously. So, if you have a zero-sum mindset, the only way to get ahead is by taking things from others. If the pie is fixed, the only way to have more pie is to take someone else's pie. But this is false, obviously, the pie has grown dramatically over time—the economic pie. In reality… there is a lot of pie. Pie is not fixed. So, you really want to make sure you're not operating, without realizing it, from a zero-sum mindset, where the only way to get ahead is to take things from others."

This is a crucial idea laid out by Musk here. Tons of people never even grasp the whole zero-sum thing—prominent people, too. You have the ability to create value (that results in money) in this world that never existed before. You don't need to take from others in order to fill your own cup, but many bend their morals while thinking otherwise.

25. IMPORTANCE OF BIRTH RATE

PRINCIPLE:

PAY ATTENTION TO BIRTH RATE.

If we do not have kids, there is no Civilization. Pay attention to the birth rate, because today it indicates that Civilization is in for a severe decline in the near future.

QUOTES:

"If the alarming collapse in birth rate continues, civilization will indeed die with a whimper in adult diapers."

—

"South Korea is currently tracking to lose about half its population roughly every generation. Long lifespan hides the dire nature of the problem."

—

"Most people still think China has a one-child policy. China had its lowest birth rate ever last year, despite having a three-child policy! At current birth rates, China will lose ~40% of people every generation! Population collapse."

—

"It takes 20 years (time from conception to adult) to reverse demographic trends."

—

"I think demographics is a real issue, where people are not having kids in a lot of countries. They'll very often say, 'Oh, I'll solve it with immigration.' Immigration from where? If Europe has an average, or many parts of Europe, have an average of only 50 or 60 percent of what's needed for replacement, or China for that matter, they're at half replacement rate; where exactly are we gonna find 600 million people to replace the ones that were never born? I think people are going to have to regard to some degree the notion of having kids as almost a social duty... within reason, if you can and you're so inclined, you should... otherwise, civilization will just die, literally. The birth rate is strongly correlated to, well it's inversely correlated to wealth, inversely correlated to education, and correlated to religion. So, the more religious you are, the less educated, and the poorer you are, the more kids you will have. This is true between countries and within countries. In the US the highest birth rate is in Utah, with the Mormons. I think that if you are saying, 'What are the threats to civilization?' The lack of people... is obviously a threat to civilization. We are going to face in the mid-part of this century and particularly the latter part of the century, a demographic implosion the likes of which we haven't seen... including the Black Plague. The math is obvious. When did China ever experience a 50% reduction in its population? Never. I mean, basically pre-writing, because no one has ever written of such a thing. Even the Black Plague... they might have lost a quarter, but never a half, and yet, Spain, a birth rate of 50%. It's as though someone went through and killed half the population, or at least of the future population. There's something that better happen to turn this around, because otherwise you have an inverted demographic pyramid [skinny on bottom, fat on top] and it's gonna [motions a collapse with his hand]. At this rate the only thing that will be left will be robots. Three generations of... 50% replacement rate, gets you to 12% of where you were. And those 12%, all they're going to be doing is taking care of their grandparents. Eventually, there just won't be people at that rate."

—

"Ratio of retirees to workers is tracking towards unsustainability in many countries. An upside-down demographic pyramid is unstable."

—Elon Musk

APPLICATION:

Wherever Musk can increase the longevity of Civilization, he takes action. This includes reversing a declining birth rate. At the time of writing this, he has ten kids. Musk is pushing humanity to get to Mars, transitioning humanity to sustainable energy, safeguarding against the danger of AI, solving the traffic problem, protecting free speech, and also carving out time to be a good father. Obviously, the Musk family is a bit different than most, but he says he does get to spend a significant amount of time with his kids. Musk's kids will often travel with him. Although many believe otherwise, his kids are a huge part of his life:

> "I always try to reserve time for my kids because I love hanging out with them. Kids are really great. I mean, 99% of the time, they make you happier… Of anything in my life, I would say kids by far make me the happiest. A lot of times, kids are kind of in their

own worlds. They don't want to talk to their dad for hours on end, generally. So, I can be in the same room with them, they can talk to me from time to time, but I can get some emails done, get some work done, and then whenever they want to talk to me, they can."

If anyone could make the career-over-kids argument, it would be Musk, yet he's doing both.

26. PREREQUISITE TO ATTRACT GREAT PEOPLE

PRINCIPLE:

ATTRACT HIGH-QUALITY PEOPLE BY DEVELOPING DEEP CONVICTION.

In order to attract high-quality people as a leader, you must build deep conviction within yourself. This conviction is a result of your diligent effort to seek out truth and understand the nature of things. Only those who are confident in their ideas will be followed by the best people.

QUOTES:

"Really believe in what you're doing, but not just from a blind faith standpoint, but like, to have really thought about it and say, 'OK, this is true, I am convinced this is true and I've tried every angle to figure out if it's untrue and sort negative feedback to figure out if I may be wrong, but then after all of that… OK, it still seems like this is the right way to go.' Then that gives one a fundamental conviction and an ability to convey that conviction to others and to convince them to join."

—

"In order to recruit the best people, I think you have to have a very compelling goal for the company. If you put yourself in the shoes of someone who, say, is at the 'world level,' then they're going to want to do something that really makes a difference… So, they have to believe that this [your startup] is going to have potential for a great outcome and they have to believe in whoever the leader of the company is. So, it's critical that you convince them that you're the right guy to work with and that can be a very difficult thing, particularly when you're trying to attract people from existing companies, because then you're trying to convince them that they should leave something which is a relatively sure thing for the uncertainty of a startup… So, they have to believe that it's going to be interesting, that it's going to change the world and that their efforts will be rewarded financially—that [financial reward] is arguably the least important but that still should be a factor."

—

"Tesla believes strongly in making things. They [Google and Apple] do not. That's fine; it's a philosophical difference. We believe that manufacturing technology is itself subject to a tremendous amount of innovation, and in fact, we believe that there's more potential for innovation in manufacturing than there is in the design of a car by a long shot. This is just a philosophical difference. Perhaps we are wrong. But we believe in manufacturing, and we believe that a company that values manufacturing as highly as we do is going to attract the best minds in manufacturing."

—

"In general, if you want to recruit people who are really talented and driven you have to state: 'What's the mission? What's the problem we're trying to solve?' And just be clearly willing to pour a lot of blood, sweat, and tears into it and have a convincing argument for why it matters."

—Elon Musk

APPLICATION:

In 2008, when Tesla was hemorrhaging money and was on the verge of bankruptcy, Musk's largest investor informed him that they were not going to put another penny into the company. In response, Musk put his money where his conviction was. Steve Jurvetson, a man who has invested over $100 million into the

Musk family of companies, witnessed something extraordinary during that time period:

> "In that moment, Elon did something that I've never seen any entrepreneur do. Going net into debt, he borrowed money from friends, literally spent every penny he had, plus more, and he told all the folks at Tesla that 'I'll just do the whole thing. I'll invest $40 million.' He had no house to his name, he had nothing… he was all in. And what happened was people's fear switched to greed. All the other inside investors, ourselves included, invested as much as we could. That wasn't our bravery; that was Elon's bravery that we attached to. Part of it I think comes from a self-affirming nature that his brother Kimbal described as being somewhat immune to risk. A more accurate description is that he so truly sees the vision of what's unfolding that it doesn't seem fathomable that it would not happen."

Jurvetson's words are spot on. Although Musk is often considered insane, in reality, Musk is usually the most sane person in the room; he's just thinking from first principles (Principle 3) and zooming out (Principle 41) to see the big picture and the fundamental truths. He builds conviction on clear insights. Once he has built that strong conviction, he's able to attract other top-notch people—including smart employees and investors, like Jurvetson. If Musk hadn't led Tesla in this way through 2008, the company would be dead. Musk's conviction attracted a great team of people who kept it alive.

Last but not least—per the first quote in this chapter, there's a difference between conviction and blind faith. Blind faith might look like conviction on the surface. But unlike solid conviction, blind faith is quickly exposed and invalidated when it doesn't correspond to reality. Rallying people around blind faith is a short-sighted plan because you'll lose their support as soon as your beliefs fail to match how the world really is. Only through learning and reasoning diligently can you arrive at the truth, and the truth is at the core of every excellent leader's conviction. Musk has spent a great deal of time deciphering the truth in all his pursuits. He dedicates immense brain energy in pursuit of truth, and always has:

"I was just absolutely obsessed with truth [as a kid]. The obsession with truth is why I studied physics, because physics attempts to understand the truth of the universe. Physics is just what are the provable truths of the universe and truths that have predictive power."

When you uncover and understand the truth, you have ground to plant your feet upon, and you are then capable of leading those who stand on shaky ground.

27. GOLDEN AGE OF LEVERAGE

PRINCIPLE:

TAKE ADVANTAGE OF LEVERAGE.

Do everything you can to take advantage of the leverage offered by software and media in this digital age. There has never been a time in history when the average human has had more leverage, so don't waste the opportunity.

QUOTES:

> "We are already a cyborg. You have a digital version of yourself or partial version of yourself online in the form of your emails and your social media and all the things that you do. And you have, basically, superpowers with your computer and your phone and the applications that are there. You have more

power than the president of the United States had 20 years ago. You can answer any question, you can video conference with anyone anywhere, you can send a message to millions of people instantly. You can just do incredible things."

—

"The thing about the internet, if you've got even a low-cost device and low-cost access to the internet, you can learn anything. MIT for example, I believe their lectures are available for free on YouTube. So, you can learn practically anything for free on the internet, provided you have internet access and at least some level of education to allow you to learn more from the internet."

—

"Computers are absurdly more accurate than humans. How long would it take for a human to render even one frame of a modern video game at low res? The computer will do high res at 120 frames per second. Not a contest."

—

"I didn't have any money, so I thought we've got to make something that's going to return money very, very quickly. We thought the media industry would need help converting its contents from print media to electronic, and they clearly had money. If we could find a way to help them move their media to the internet, that would be an obvious way of generating revenue. There was no advertising revenue on the internet at the time. That was really the basis of Zip2."

—Elon Musk

APPLICATION:

A simple way of understanding leverage: the ability to influence a system, situation, or environment in a way that multiplies the initial efforts you put in. You get a lot of output from a comparatively small amount of input.

Musk by luck (or fate) developed an extremely high-leverage skill early on. The first time he saw a computer was when he was 10. He was instantly hooked. He convinced his father to buy a Commodore VIC-20. The classic computer came with five kilobytes of memory… and a programming book on the BASIC coding language. The booklet was supposed to last six months, but Musk got to work right away: "I just got super OCD on it and stayed up for three days with no sleep and did the entire thing. It seemed like the most super-compelling thing I had ever seen."

Shortly after learning how to code, he made a rudimentary game called Blastar and sold it. This story is an early microcosm of Musk's future: high drive + engineering = value creation.

The strong coding abilities Musk developed gave him the opportunity to ride the wave of the internet later down the road. The first two companies he built were both internet companies and involved a lot of coding. Zip2 and PayPal grew extraordinarily fast in comparison to traditional brick-and-mortar businesses. In an interview, Musk said: "If it was about money, I'd just do another internet company."

In other words, if he wanted to simply accumulate wealth in the shortest amount of time possible, he would pursue code and digital content.^ϕ That statement says it all right there.

ϕ The reason you are reading this book is because of a Twitter account and a tweet I sent out mentioning Musk's account handle. Don't underestimate the power in the palm of your hand. Take advantage of the Golden Age of Leverage!

28. DANGER OF AI

PRINCIPLE:

EDUCATE YOURSELF ON
ARTIFICIAL INTELLIGENCE (AND
ESPECIALLY THE DANGERS).

AI has the potential to be very good, but also very bad. The future of AI (and humanity) largely depends on how the technology is developed. Make an effort at the very least to understand what is going on and, ideally, participate in the safe development of the technology in whatever way you can.

QUOTES:

"I have exposure to the very most cutting-edge AI, and I think people should be really concerned about it.

I keep sounding the alarm bell but until people see robots going down the street killing people they don't know how to react because it seems so ethereal."

—

"Digital super-intelligence, I think, has the potential to be more dangerous than a nuclear bomb, so somebody should be keeping an eye [on it]. We can't have the inmates running the asylum."

—

"AI is a fundamental existential risk for human civilization and I don't think people fully appreciate that."

—

"It's not as though I think that the risk is that the AI would develop a will of its own right off the bat. The concern is that someone may use it in a way that is bad, and even if they weren't going to use it in a way that is bad, somebody could take it from them and use it in a way that's bad. That, I think, is quite a big danger. So, I think we must have a democratization of AI technology and make it widely available. That's the reason [we] created OpenAI."

—

"The safety of any AI system can be measured by its MtH (meantime to Hitler). Microsoft's Tay chatbot of several years ago got there in ~24 hours."

———

"I was just pointing out with the anthill analogy that AI does not need to hate us to destroy us. In a sense, that if it decides that it needs to go in a particular direction and we're in the way then it would, with no hard feelings, it would just roll over us. We would roll over an anthill that's in the way of a road. You don't hate ants. You're just building a road. It's a risk not a prediction. So, yeah. I think that we really need to think of intelligence as really not being uniquely confined to humans. And that the potential for intelligence in computers is far greater than in biology."

———

"It feels like we are the biological boot loader for AI, effectively. We are building it. And then, we're building progressively greater intelligence, and the percentage of intelligence that is not human is increasing, and eventually, we will represent a very small percentage of intelligence."

———

"My view on AI is essentially, you can view the advancement of AI as solving things with increasing degrees of freedom. So, the thing with the most degrees of freedom is reality. But AI has steadily advanced, solving things that have more and more degrees of freedom. So, obviously, something like checkers was very easy to solve, that you could solve with classical software, classical computing… every version of checkers is known. And then there's chess, which also had many, many more degrees of freedom than checkers. Many orders of magnitude more than checkers. But still really, I would say it's a lower order of magnitude, lower degree of freedom game. Then there's Go, which had many orders of magnitude more degrees of freedom than chess. So, it's really just stepping through orders of magnitude of degrees of freedom. This is the way to, I think, view the advancement of intelligence. And is really going to get to the point where it just can completely simulate a person in every way possible."

—

"[AI] could be terrible, and it could be great. It's not clear. But one thing is for sure: We will not control it."

—Elon Musk

APPLICATION:

For this principle, we are going to discuss Neuralink—the potential solution to the potential AI problem. Musk founded Neuralink in 2016. Today in 2023, AI is becoming more and more sophisticated: it's creating art, mimicking human voices, and even creating realistic podcasts. Clearly, we are heading in a direction in which AI has tremendous power. It is likely going to get to the point where AI becomes dangerously powerful. An important note: AI doesn't have to become self-conscious to wipe us out; it just has to fall into the wrong human hands. You may be wondering how an AI disaster may play out. Here's a potential unfolding from Musk:

> "The thing that is most dangerous is… and it's the hardest to kind of wrap… to get your arms around, because it's not a physical thing; it's a deep intelligence in the network. You might say, 'What harm could a deep intelligence in the network do?' Well, it could start a war… by doing fake news and spoofing email accounts and fake press releases… and just by manipulating information. 'The pen is mightier than the sword.'"

Musk's solution to avoid doom by AI is to offer a symbiosis between machine and man:

> "I think one of the solutions [to the threat of Godlike general AI]—the solution that seems maybe the best one—is to have an AI layer. If you think, you've got your limbic system, your cortex, and then a digital

layer—sort of a third layer above the cortex that could work well and symbiotically with you, just as your cortex works symbiotically with your limbic system, a third digital layer could work symbiotically with the rest of you."

His intention with Neuralink is to democratize AI technology. By making the power of AI available to all, it removes the ability for a small minority to wield all the power. And in the case that AI develops by itself and humans can't control it, at least we may be spared if we can access the power, too. Neuralink's tagline is: "If you can't beat 'em, join 'em." AI is coming, but how it's coming is the question. Due to this uncertainty, we should try to put ourselves in the best possible position to survive the revolutionary event. Neuralink is a potential answer.

This idea may freak you out… and rightly so, but it's important to keep in mind that Neuralink's progress will be fairly slow (hopefully not too slow, if it's truly our best hope of facing an advanced artificial general intelligence). Their progress will be slowed down by the large regulatory apparatuses that approve medical devices. Lastly, it's important to keep in mind that the symbiosis of man and machine has already occurred more or less—from Musk's point of view: "You already are symbiotic with AI or computers… It's just a question of your data rate. The communication between your phone and your brain is slow."

How often have you left to go somewhere and realized you forgot your phone? It feels like you're missing a limb or something. But, even if we are heavily connected to our devices, our data rate is severely limited (compared to a computer). Our data rate is capped, more or less, by how fast our thumbs can tap a screen. Neuralink is working (under extreme scrutiny) to bridge that gap.

29. AT THE END OF THE DAY, IT'S PEOPLE

PRINCIPLE:

SURROUND YOURSELF WITH PEOPLE OF THE HIGHEST QUALITY (ACROSS THE BOARD).

Companies, organizations, clubs, troupes, platoons, and families are just groups of people, so make sure the quality of the people you assemble is high. The quality of what you offer and the magnitude of your impact are directly correlated to the quality of the people in your groups.

QUOTES:

"The biggest mistake in general that I've made—and I'm trying to correct for that—is to put too much of a weighting on somebody's talent and not enough on their personality… It actually matters whether somebody has a good heart, it really does. And I've made the mistake of thinking that sometimes it's just about the brain."

—

"The ability to attract and motivate great people is critical to the success of a company because a company is just a group of people that are assembled to create a product or service… People sometimes forget this elementary truth. If you're able to get great people to join the company and work together toward a common goal and have a relentless sense of perfection about that goal, then you will end up with a great product. And if you have a great product, lots of people will buy it, and then the company will be successful."

—

"Talent is extremely important. It's really just like a sports team; the team that will win is the one that has the best individual players, but then there's a multiplier from how well those players work together and the strategy that they employ collectively."

—

"We have a strict no-assholes policy at SpaceX… we give them a little bit of a warning, but if they continue to be an asshole, then they're fired… If your boss is an awful person, you're going to hate coming to work."

—

"Technology leadership is not defined by patents, which history has repeatedly shown to be small protection indeed against a determined competitor, but rather by the ability of a company to attract and motivate the world's most talented engineers."

—

"If you have a choice of a lower valuation with someone you really like or a higher valuation with someone you have a question mark about, take the lower valuation. It's better to have a higher quality venture capitalist who you think would be great to work with than to get a higher valuation with someone where there's even a question mark, really."

—

"Output of any company is the vector sum of people within it. Someone may be a strong vector, but negatively affect those around them to such a degree that they are a net negative."

—Elon Musk

APPLICATION:

Surrounding yourself with the right people is important in every dimension of life, but it's vital if you're trying to build a company. During the early days of SpaceX and Tesla, Musk interviewed every single candidate who applied. It didn't matter which position they'd applied for; he talked to them all. Musk, as you might imagine, has a tried-and-true interviewing process to filter for quality people. Here's his go-to interview question:

> "When I interview somebody, I really just ask them to tell me the story of their career and what are some of the tougher problems that they dealt with, how they dealt with those and how they made decisions at key transition points. Usually, that's enough for me to get a very good gut feel about someone. And what I'm really looking for is evidence of exceptional ability. So, did they face really difficult problems and overcome them? And of course, you want to make sure that if there was some significant accomplishment, were they really responsible or was somebody else more responsible? And usually, the person who's had to struggle with the problem, they really understand it and they don't forget, you know, if it was very difficult. You can ask them very detailed questions about it, and they will know the answer. Whereas the person who was not truly responsible for that accomplishment, will not know the details."

This approach allows you to see who the real problem solvers are. It's a bullshitter filter, essentially. When interviewees discuss their lives and the problems they've solved, it allows Musk to not only filter for competency, but also collect a strong understanding of each person's character.

There was a time when Musk didn't understand people well. He has discussed on several occasions how Asperger's has made developing people skills more challenging:

"I think everyone's experience is going to be somewhat different, but I guess for me social cues were not intuitive. So, I was just very bookish, and I guess others could intuitively understand what was meant by something… I would just tend to take things very literally, the words as spoken were exactly what they meant, but that turned out to be wrong [laughs]. They're not simply saying exactly what they mean, there's all sorts of other things that are meant. It took me a while to figure that out. So, I was bullied quite a lot. I did not have sort of a happy childhood to be frank, it was quite rough. But I read a lot of books, I read lots and lots of books and so I gradually understood more from the books I was reading and watched a lot of movies. It took me a while to understand things that most people intuitively understand."

Considering Musk primarily uses his gut to determine people's character today, he has made tremendous progress on this front. Fortunately, Musk doesn't have to involve himself so heavily in the interviewing[φ] process anymore, as he has assembled tremendous teams at all of his companies.

φ Another interesting interview question Musk would ask is: "You're standing on the surface of the Earth. You walk one mile south, one mile west, and one mile north. You end up exactly where you started. Where are you?" Do you know the answer? Think about it for a moment.
Answer: The North Pole. (or the South Pole)
This type of brain teaser aims at figuring out what kind of critical thinking skills somebody possesses while under pressure. The right answer was of less importance than seeing what an individual's thought process was like.

30. PROGRAM OR BE PROGRAMMED

PRINCIPLE:

PROGRAM YOURSELF OR SOMEONE ELSE WILL PROGRAM YOU.

Mental programming occurs constantly in modern times; make sure you're aware this is happening and you're the one writing the code. Question everything.

QUOTES:

"Who wrote the software running in your head? Are you sure you actually want it there?"

—

"The overarching problem is that we need better mental firewalls for the information constantly coming at us. Critical and first principle thinking should be a required course in middle school."

—

"In any sort of train of thinking, you want to make sure that the underlying premises are valid and applicable and then in reaching a conclusion, that the conclusion you're reaching is necessarily driven by the underlying premises and interconnection between those premises. That may seem like a really simple thing to say, but most people don't do that. It's really the foundation of rational thought."

—

"Think about who might have decided 'The Current Thing' before accepting it."

—

[worth repeating] "I do kind of feel like my head is full! My context-switching penalty is high, and my process isolation is not what it used to be. Frankly, though, I think most people can learn a lot more than they think they can. They sell themselves short without trying. One bit of advice: it is important to view knowledge as sort of a semantic tree—make sure you understand the fundamental principles, i.e., the trunk and big branches, before you get into the leaves/details or there's nothing for them to hang on to."

—Elon Musk

APPLICATION:

What's the best way to program your mind? Reading is hard to beat. This was Musk's primary approach to learning throughout his youth: "I read thousands and thousands of books." In a separate interview: "I was always sort of really interested in reading when I was a kid, and I would read everything I could get my hands on. I read the encyclopedia, probably age 9 or 10." Musk read the entire encyclopedia because he ran out of books at his local library. This wasn't about aiming to get good grades or impress teachers. In fact, fixating on grades would've meant accepting the default social programming, which Musk has never been about. He paid attention to his grades mostly from a practical standpoint:

> "I just look at it as 'What grades do I need to get where I want to go?' There were compulsory subjects like Afrikaans, and I just didn't see the point of learning that. It seemed ridiculous. I'd get a passing grade and that was fine. Things like physics and computers—I got the highest grade you can get in those. There needs to be a reason for a grade. I'd rather play video games, write software, and read books than try and get an A if there's no point in getting an A. I can remember failing

subjects in like fourth and fifth grade, then my mother's boyfriend told me I'd be held back if I didn't pass. I didn't actually know you had to pass a subject to move to the next grade. I got the best grades in class after that."

Musk read and learned because he wanted to nourish his mind and understand the world for himself. He didn't let other people tell him what to think or what to prioritize in his learning. This is a huge deal. Hardly anyone takes the time to curate their education intentionally. This results in them being used by others as a human battery of sorts. You do not want to be laying on your death bed and come to the realization that you lived your entire life for someone else's soulless desires, or through programming that wasn't your own.

This ability to self-program ϕ that Musk developed early on helped him breeze through school and later excel in the business world.

ϕ Biographies can offer an immense return on investment. Musk is a big fan of biographies because of the distilled knowledge within them. He has mentioned Isaacson's biographies as some of his favorites, especially the one on Benjamin Franklin. (Pretty crazy that Isaacson is now writing a biography on Musk!) I myself have been affected by biographies so profoundly that I started a project called The Knowledge Archivist on Twitter in an effort to share useful knowledge I've gained from studying the great people of history.

31.

THE NATURE OF SOCIAL MEDIA

PRINCIPLE:

SOCIAL MEDIA IS NOT REAL LIFE.

Social media is largely a mirror—it can amplify both the good and bad of human nature. But it's important to recognize that it doesn't always accurately represent reality. This false reality can negatively impact your psychological well-being, so stay vigilant and make consistent efforts to curate an experience online that aids you in your life rather than hinders you.

QUOTES:

"One of the issues with social media, and it's been pointed out by many people, is that... I think particularly Instagram, people look like they have a much better life than they really do. People are posting pictures of when they're really happy, they're modifying those pictures to be better looking, even if they're not modifying the pictures, they're at least selecting the pictures for the best lighting, the best angle... so people basically seem way better looking than they really are and they're way happier seeming than they really are. So, if you look at everyone on Instagram you might think, 'Man, there's all these happy, beautiful people and I'm not that good looking and I'm not happy, so I must suck.' You know, that's gonna make people sad, when in fact, those people you think are super happy, actually, not that happy, some of them are really depressed... Some of the happiest-seeming people are actually some of the saddest people in reality."

—

"It's way easier to be mean on social media than it is to be mean in person."

—

"Instagram is an envy amplifier."

—Elon Musk

APPLICATION:

Musk is human, so he's also vulnerable to the dangers of social media. Musk is solely on Twitter and nowhere else. He believes he only needs one place to get his word out. At one time he had a public Instagram, but he has since deleted it. He's not a huge fan of Instagram: "The problem with Instagram, man, is it's just a thirst trap, you know? Instagram is a next-level thirst trap... and the thing is, is I found myself taking a lot of selfies and shit, and I'm like what the fuck man... why am I doing this?" Everyone has experienced the dopamine hits that accompany social media sites. Some are worse than others.

Musk has been on Twitter for a long time and has over 135 million followers (probably more when you read this). His long presence on the app and its general town-square nature are among the reasons Musk ended up buying Twitter. Just before buying the app, he laid out some of his thoughts regarding its potential in a recent interview:

> "I think it's very important for there to be an inclusive arena for free speech. Twitter has become kind of the de facto town square, so it's really important that people have both the reality and the perception that they are able to speak freely within the bounds of the law. So, one of the things that I think Twitter should do is open-source the algorithm and make any changes to people's tweets, you know, if they're emphasized or de-emphasized, that action should be made apparent so anyone can see that action has been taken. So, there's no sort of behind-the-scenes manipulation either algorithmically or manually."

In the same interview, Chris Anderson of TEDx asked Musk why he would want to partake in the likely miserable experience of running Twitter. Musk responded:

> "It's important to the function of democracy, it's important to the function of the United States as a free country and many other countries, and to actually help freedom in the world, more broadly than the US... the civilizational risk is decreased the more that we can increase the trust of Twitter as a public platform."

Musk's primary motive for acquiring the app is tied to the well-being of Civilization, like all his companies.

With the purchase of Twitter, Musk is attempting to reorder this social media experiment. He intends to build an app that facilitates well-being. This is an incredibly exciting development in the tech industry and for the world in general. We finally ⏀ have someone fighting for the things that make Civilization great.

⏀ Get on Twitter!

32. ON FEAR

PRINCIPLE:

FEAR = FALSE EVIDENCE APPEARING REAL

Fear is often an illusion that keeps you in your comfort zone. The cautious often survived as we continued to evolve. But to do great things you need to muster the courage to continue in spite of those feelings. Let meaning and purpose propel you.

QUOTES:

"I think people sometimes are afraid of things when they shouldn't be afraid of things. Like you want to make sure that your fear is proportionate to the actual danger. Sometimes our instinctive fear is not proportionate to the actual danger. So, you want to try to rethink things and say, 'OK, is that fear justified? Will something bad actually happen?' You sort of have to sometimes look at your instinctive fear and question it and decide whether that is really a valid fear or not and often it is not, and simply looking at the fear will make it go away."

—

"People shouldn't think, 'Well, I feel fear about this and therefore I shouldn't do it.' It's normal to feel fear; there would have to be something mentally wrong with you if you didn't feel fear."

—

"It is not as though I have the absence of fear; I feel it quite strongly. But there are times when something is important enough, you believe in it enough, that you do it in spite of the fear."

—

"People tend to overweight risk on a personal level. It's one thing if you've got a mortgage to pay and kids to support and if you were to deviate from your job, well how're you going to feed your family and pay the rent… Okay, that's understandable but let's say you're young and just coming out of college or coming out of high school… What do you risk? You're not going to starve, certainly not in any modern economy, it's so easy to earn enough money to just live somewhere and eat food, it's very easy to do. So, what are they afraid of? They're mostly afraid of failure, I think… people should be less risk averse when there's not much at risk…"

———

"Anything which is significantly innovative is going to come with a significant risk of failure. But you know, you've got to take big chances in order for the potential for a big positive outcome. If the outcome is exciting enough, then taking a big risk is worthwhile… that's really how I approach it, but then once executing down a path I do my absolute best to reduce risk."

———

"Something that can be helpful is fatalism, to some degree. If you just accept the probabilities, then that diminishes fear. Starting SpaceX, I thought the odds of success were less than 10% and I just accepted that probability… I would just lose everything but that maybe we would make some progress… if we could just move the ball forward, even if we died, maybe some other company could pick up the baton and keep moving it forward so that will still do some good. Same with Tesla, I thought the odds of a car company succeeding were extremely low."

———

"Accept worst-case outcome and assign it a probability, which is usually very low. Now think of good things in life and assign them probabilities—many are certain! Bringing anxiety/fear to the conscious mind saps it of limbic emotional strength. Cheery fatalism is very effective."

—

"I was at a lunch with Munger in 2009 where he told the whole table all the ways Tesla would fail. Made me quite sad, but I told him I agreed with all those reasons and that we would probably die, but it was worth trying anyway."

—

"There's been many times where I expected to lose everything. I mean, who starts a car company and a rocket company expecting them to succeed? Certainly not me, I thought they both had less than a 10% chance of success... If I go bankrupt, fine, whatever. I don't care."

—

"Failure is essentially irrelevant unless it is catastrophic."

—Elon Musk

APPLICATION:

Musk isn't one to fall for fear's trickery. He was born and raised in South Africa. But he didn't enjoy his time in the country, as it was a violent place and offered little to no opportunity regarding technology. As his brother Kimbal put it: "South Africa was like a prison for someone like Elon." Musk's goal was to ultimately make it to Silicon Valley. He ended up deciding to move to Canada first, because of his Canadian ancestry. Unfortunately, the process of moving to Canada was long, and to avoid serving in the military under the apartheid regime, he chose to attend the University of Pretoria for five months while he waited for his Canadian documentation. During his brief stint at the University of Pretoria, a law changed which allowed Musk's mother, Maye Musk, to pass her Canadian citizenship to her children. Musk went into full research mode figuring out how to complete the paperwork needed to gain citizenship. It took nearly a year to hear back from the Canadian government, but they eventually granted him a passport. Musk immediately told his mother: "I'm leaving for Canada."

After three weeks, he received his plane ticket and left South Africa without hesitation. Musk had planned on staying with a great-uncle once he arrived in Montreal. But when he landed, he called his great-uncle from a payphone and received no answer. He phoned his mother, and she informed him that the uncle had sent them a letter while Musk was in transit saying that he had moved to Minnesota... not good. This didn't deter Musk, though; he simply headed for the nearest youth hostel. He eventually took a bus out to his second cousin's farm, which was about 1,900 miles away from Montreal. He spent a year in the area working a number of odd jobs. One of the most brutal jobs Musk worked was cleaning out the boiler room of a lumber mill. He made $18 an hour working that job (in a hazmat suit). In 1989, he enrolled at Queen's University in Kingston, Ontario. He only spent two years there before transferring to the University of Pennsylvania where he received bachelor's degrees in physics and economics. From there he went to Stanford to pursue a graduate degree—but after a few days in the program, he dropped out to launch his first startup, Zip2.

The vast majority of people would not take the risk that Musk did in moving from South Africa to Canada. Musk was not 100% guaranteed anything—shelter, safety, contacts, or comfort—but he took the leap anyway. Musk's motto for approaching risk and fear is this: "I feel fear quite strongly. But if what we're doing is important then I just override the fear."

Easier said than done. But if you analyze the fear thoroughly, the feelings will diminish, as many of our fears are irrational and more rooted in evolutionary drives than situational facts.

33. CHAOS AND ORDER

PRINCIPLE:

UNDERSTAND LIFE'S TENDENCY
TO MOVE TOWARD ENTROPY.

In life, the two most fundamental forces are chaos and order. Life and human behavior tend toward chaos. You must actively seek order to avoid getting lost in the chaos.

QUOTES:

> "Things move as fast as the least lucky and least competent supplier. Any natural disaster you care to name—all of those things have happened to our suppliers. The factory has burned down, there's been an earthquake, there's been a tsunami, there's been massive hail, there's been a tornado, the ship sank,

there was a shoot-out at the Mexican border—no kidding, that delayed trunk carpet at one point. The border patrol wouldn't give us the truck because it had bullet holes in it."

—

"Simplify your product as much as possible. If you think of some of the ways in which—how does a smart engineer, make dumb mistakes? You optimize something that shouldn't exist. Don't optimize something that shouldn't exist."

—

"One of the most fundamental errors made in advanced development is to stick to a design even when it is very complicated and to not strive to delete parts and processes."

—

"If the schedule is long, the design is wrong. We've overcomplicated the design many times and I think we should have just gone with a simpler design [rocket]. With the acid test being: 'How long will it take for this to fly?' If it's going to take a long time, don't do it. Do something else."

—

"In the end it's all about entropy."

—Elon Musk

APPLICATION:

The physics definition of entropy: "A thermodynamic quantity representing the unavailability of a system's thermal energy for conversion into mechanical work, often interpreted as the degree of disorder or randomness in the system."

Simpler definition: lack of order or predictability; decline into disorder.

Entropy is visible in the ultra-exacting space industry. The first rocket SpaceX created was the Falcon 1. The rocket is a two-stage launch vehicle with the capability of putting a metric ton (1000 kg) into Earth's low orbit. The Falcon 1 rocket featured one single Merlin engine, which produced ~570,000 newtons of thrust. An apt comparison: a single Shuttle main engine produces about 2,300,000 newtons of thrust. This was a relatively small rocket, but that doesn't mean it's not still unbelievably difficult to build.

Musk said this about building and launching rockets:

"There is some entropic basis to this [failure]. There are many more ways to fail than to succeed. Particularly for a rocket, there are a thousand ways the thing can fail and one way it can work. You could have a lot of rocket failures to explore all the ways in which it could fail. But I do think that one great thing about Silicon Valley is that failure is not a big stigma. It's like if you try hard and it doesn't work out, that's OK. You can learn from that and do another company, and it's not a big deal."

On March 24, 2006, SpaceX launched the Falcon 1. The result of the launch: failure. It had taken them 6 years to build the rocket and within 25 seconds, their precious hard work erupted in flames. The cause of this failure was due to a single seal leak. They had built the rocket on a small island in the Pacific, and the salty air had corroded one single aluminum nut. The faulty nut resulted in a fuel leak and a fire broke out. The fire then produced a loss of pressure that shut down the engine. One. Single. Nut.

The next two launches of Falcon 1 also failed due to exceedingly minor errors. The company had only planned for 3 flights but ended up being able to scrape enough resources together for a fourth launch. If this fourth launch failed, SpaceX would die. What change did they make to the fourth rocket? They made one software alteration (one more bit of order). The life of the company was on the line with this last launch. On September 28, 2008, they launched for the fourth time; success.

34. THE NATURE OF ENTREPRENEURSHIP

PRINCIPLE:

ENTREPRENEURSHIP IS EXTREMELY HARD.

It is great if you want to run a business, but understand that it will be difficult, painful, and taxing (literally). Difficulty and entrepreneurship go hand in hand.

QUOTES:

"Generally starting a business, I'd say #1 is have a high pain threshold."

—

"There's a friend of mine who says: 'Starting a company is like staring into the abyss and eating glass' and there's some truth to that. The staring into the abyss part is that you're going to be constantly facing the extermination of the company… because most startups fail. It's like 90%, arguably 99% of startups fail. So, that's the staring into the abyss part, you're constantly saying 'OK, if I don't get this right, the company will die which can be quite stressful. And then the eating glass part is… you've got to work on the problems that the company needs you to work on and not the problems you wanna work on. And so, you end up working on problems that you really wish you weren't working on… so, that's the eating glass part and that goes on for a long time."

—

"A lot of times people think creating a company is going to be fun. I would say it's not, it's really not that fun. There are periods of fun, and there are periods where it's just awful. Particularly if you're the CEO of the company, you actually have a distillation of all the worst problems in the company. There's no point in spending your time on things that are going right, so you only spend your time on things that are going wrong, and they are things that are going wrong that other people can't take care of… you have a filter for the crappest [sic] problems in the company, the most pernicious and painful problems. So, I think you have to feel quite compelled to do it and have a very high pain threshold."

—

"I would definitely advise people who are starting a company to expect a long period of quite high difficulty."

—

"I think it's very difficult to start companies and quite painful. That's important to bear in mind. That's probably not encouraging... If you go into it expecting it's just fun, you will be disappointed; it's not, it's quite painful. It's much easier to get a job somewhere, much, much easier... much less stressful, you'll have more time for other things... It's really like if you're sort of wired to do it, then you should do it, but not otherwise. It's not going to optimize your leisure time or anything like that, it's going to be extremely difficult and stressful, so you must feel compelled to do it. Think of it this way: if you need inspiring words—don't do it."

—

"The hard part of solar power is not the panel. It's actually the whole system. It's basically designing something that's going to fit on a particular rooftop... Then you've got to mount the system, you've got to wire it up, you've got to connect the inverters to the grid, you've got to do all the permitting… It's a bunch of thorny, unglamorous, stupid problems, but if somebody doesn't optimize them, they're still going to cost a ton of money. And a lot of them are not fun problems. They're not exciting problems to optimize, but they are the problems that actually matter in the cost of solar power."

—

"My advice, if somebody wants to start a company is they should bear in mind that the most likely outcome is that it's not going to work, and they should reconcile themselves to that strong possibility. And they should only do it if they feel that they're really compelled to do it."

—

"Starting a business is not for everyone."

—Elon Musk

APPLICATION:

Since we already covered Musk's entrepreneurial suffering and the principle was clarified well in the quotes, the focus here will be on one of the most advantageous ways to combat the difficulty of entrepreneurship.

When Musk was attending Queen's University in Ontario, Canada, he would scan newspapers for interesting people to contact. He would then do his best to find ways to connect with them. He read an article about a man named Peter Nicholson, who at the time was an executive at the Bank of Nova Scotia. Nicholson has a unique background in computing, operations, and physics. According to Jimmy Soni, who wrote The Founders, which detailed the founding of PayPal, Musk thought: "He was a giant brain, just super smart." So, Musk ended up contacting Nicholson and landed a meeting with him. Nicholson offered him an internship, and Musk joined the bank. Nicholson ran a smaller team within the bank that was tasked with handling interesting problems that the CEO passed on to them.

Because the team was small, Nicholson and Musk were able to form a strong friendship. They got along well because of their shared interests. Musk and Nicholson would trade math problems and puzzles, and talk about space exploration and physics. Nicholson also provided advice regarding Musk's future. They discussed whether it made sense for Musk to try to find a job, continue school, or start a company. It was during these years that Musk saw the reality of the banking industry and the potential for disruption. Without that internship and the guidance ⊕ Nicholson offered to Musk, it's hard to say whether PayPal or even Musk himself would have seen the success they ultimately did. Every brick laid on the bridge of success matters to the completion of the project.

ⱷ If you look at the lives of ultra-successful people, you'll often see a pattern of mentor/mentee relationships. One of the best examples of this is how Socrates taught Plato, Plato taught Aristotle, and then Aristotle taught Alexander the Great. Also, it's worth repeating: read biographies—some of the greatest mentors are dead!

35. READ HISTORY

PRINCIPLE:

READ HISTORY. SERIOUSLY, DO IT.

If you study history, you will see patterns. As the saying goes: it might not repeat, but it rhymes. Things happen today that are incredibly similar to what has happened in the past, since human nature hasn't changed. If you recognize these patterns, they can help you navigate your life and society at large.

QUOTES:

"The lessons of history would suggest that civilizations move in cycles. You can track that back quite far—the Babylonians, the Sumerians, followed by the Egyptians, the Romans, China. We're obviously in a very upward cycle right now and hopefully that remains the case. But it may not."

—

"This [transition to sustainable energy] is being fought quite hard by the carbon producers, and they're using tactics that are very similar to what the tobacco industry used for many years... Even though the overwhelming scientific consensus was that smoking cigarettes was bad for you, they would find a few scientists that would disagree, and then they would say, 'Look, scientists disagree.' That's essentially how they would try to trick the public into thinking that smoking is not that bad."

—

"30 years ago, when 98% of scientists said smoking caused cancer, tobacco industry response was still 'scientists disagree.'"

—

"If SpaceX and other companies can lower the cost of transport to orbit and perhaps beyond, then there is a lot of potential for entrepreneurship at the destination. You can think of it like the Union Pacific Railway. Before there was the Union Pacific Railroad, it was really hard to have commerce between the west coast and the east coast. It would go by wagon or a really long sailing journey, but once there was the transport, then there were huge opportunities and now look at California, Washington state, and all the industries that have been created: Silicon Valley, Hollywood..."

—

"I was asked recently, what period of history would I prefer to be at the most and my answer was 'right now.' This is the most interesting time in history, and I read a lot of history."

—

"Compared to past, today's world is fantastic and likely will be for many decades. Just need to cover future downside risk."

—

"Read *The Story of Civilization* by Will & Ariel Durant"

—Elon Musk

APPLICATION:

One of the books that influenced Musk the most was Isaac Asimov's *Foundation* series. The book series focuses on Civilization's pattern of rising and falling. The story takes place in the future at a time of great prosperity due to a powerful Empire. However, the glory days are waning. The protagonist

Hari Seldon, a practicing mathematician, spends his life devising a theory of psychohistory. He develops it by applying mathematics to sociology: in the first book of the *Foundation* series, Asimov defines psychohistory as "that branch of mathematics which deals with the reactions of human conglomerates to fixed social and economic stimuli." He basically finds a way to predict the future of mass populations with accuracy based on statistical laws.

Using his theory, Seldon can see that the fall of the Empire is coming. Following their current set of actions, he determines that they will experience a Dark Age lasting 30,000 years before a new Empire rises. Although the momentum of the Empire's fall is too strong to stop, Seldon discovers a way to make the difficult period last only 1,000 years.

Musk thinks about long term probabilities, too, and makes his own life decisions accordingly. We'll touch on that principle more specifically later, but the important thing to understand now is the fundamental nature of Civilization. Civilization rises and falls. Progress isn't inevitable. If you know history, you know this. Musk flat-out tweeted: "The course of civilization is not always upward." And he's spot on. Ultimately, we want to extend the times of prosperity for as long as possible and decrease the time spent in the Dark Ages to the best of our abilities. But we can't do these things if we haven't studied history. [φ]

φ Two great history podcasts are *Hardcore History* by Dan Carlin and *Revolutions* by Mike Duncan. Musk has recommended both of these podcasts.

36. NO ONE IS 100% SELF-MADE

PRINCIPLE:

ACKNOWLEDGE THE EFFORTS OF OTHERS.

Praise and express gratitude to those who have helped you get to where you are. Without others' help, you would be nothing. Praise and acknowledgment are fuel for the soul.

QUOTES:

> "I just want to emphasize that sometimes—in fact, most of the time—I get way too much credit or attention for what I do. I'm just a visible element. But the reason those companies are successful is because we have extremely talented people at all levels that are making it happen."

—

"Shout out to the awesome Tesla global team. Thanks for working so hard to make Tesla successful!"

—

"Lots of Tesla cars to deliver before year end! Your support in taking delivery is much appreciated. Thanks also to the Tesla team working hard during the holidays!"

—

"Thanks [AI expert, Andrej Karpathy, 2022] for everything you have done for Tesla! It has been an honor working with you."

—

"Super fired up for future product development with our awesome Tesla team! Such an honor to work with them."

—

"Super proud of Tesla team for great execution and support of Tesla customers greatly appreciated!!"

—

"Tesla team is awesome, such an honor to work with them!"

—

"Incredibly proud of the SpaceX team for achieving this milestone [first to re-fly a rocket] in space! Next goal is reflight within 24 hours."

—

"Congrats to SpaceX team on 48th launch this year! Falcon 9 now holds record for most launches of a single vehicle type in a year."

—

"SpaceX team is doing great work! One day, the true measure of success will be that Starship flights are commonplace."

—

"Very proud of the SpaceX team! Can't believe it's been fifty Falcon 9 launches already. Just ten years ago, we couldn't even reach orbit with little Falcon 1."

—

"Tesla Team has done incredibly well, despite extremely difficult times. Could not be more proud of them."

—

"The failures are mine; the successes belong to others."

—Elon Musk

APPLICATION:

Musk is constantly praising his teams. But, what really stands out are the non-verbal efforts he makes to show his appreciation for those who put in an honest day's work. The product launches and company parties, for example, show Musk's care for his employees. He understands how difficult the missions are and how hard his employees work, so when it's time to showcase their work or celebrate, he goes all out. Recently, in April of 2022, Tesla held a Cyber Rodeo event in Austin, TX, to celebrate the grand opening of the Gigafactory there. This event was more or less a giant party—laser lights, exhilarating music, cool futuristic aesthetics, etc. Even watching the event through a screen at home, you could feel the excitement in the air. This event blows other companies' events out of the water. Of course, any leader can praise their team (although many don't even do that properly), but it's a rare leader who goes out of his way to make sure that unforgettable events instill workers with pride. Musk is one of these leaders.

37. ON INNOVATION

PRINCIPLE:

STUDY INNOVATION.

The degree to which you understand the nature of innovation largely determines the degree to which you lead or follow, especially in the business world.

QUOTES:

"If a design is taking too long, the design is wrong and therefore the design must be modified to accelerate progress."

—

"You get paid in direct proportion to the difficulty of the problems you solve."

—

"It's important to create an environment that fosters innovation, but you want to let it evolve in a Darwinian way. You don't want to, at a high level, at a gut level, pick a technology and decide that that's the thing that's going to win because it may not be. You should really let things evolve."

—

"Well, I think I am not actually a fan of disruption for its own sake. I think that if there is a need for something to be disrupted, and it's important to the future of the world, then sure, then we should disrupt it. I don't think we should just disrupt things unless that disruption is going to result in something fundamentally better for society. A lot of people think I am a fan of disruption. I am not really a fan of disruption. I'm just a fan of things being better."

—

"In general, I do think it's worth thinking about whether what you're doing is going to result in a disruptive change or not. If it's just incremental, it's unlikely to be something major. It's got to be something that's substantially better than what's gone on before." [if operating within an established industry]

—

"When it's a radically new product, people don't know that they want it because it's just not in their scope. When they first started making TVs, they did a nationwide survey, I think this might have been like '46 or '48, like this famous nationwide survey; 'Will you ever buy a TV?' and like 96% of respondents said 'No.'"

—

"The real way I think you actually achieve intellectual property protection is by innovating fast enough. If your rate of innovation is high, then you don't need to worry about protecting the IP because other companies will be copying something that you did years ago... speed of innovation is what matters. And I do say this to my team quite a lot: 'Innovation per unit time, innovation per year' if you will, is what matters. Not innovation absent time, because if you wanted to make say, 100% improvement in something and that took 100 years or 1 year, that's radically different. What is your rate of innovation? That matters. And is the rate of innovation, is that accelerating or decelerating?"

—

"Innovation comes from questioning the way things have been done before and if in the education system, you're taught not to do that, that will inhibit entrepreneurship."

—

"If it's a new industry or untapped market... the standard is lower for your product or service. But if you're entering anything where there is an existing marketplace against large, entrenched competitors, then your product or service needs to be much better than theirs. It can't be a little bit better, because then you put yourself in the shoes of the consumer... you're always going to buy the trusted brand unless there's a big difference."

—

"The only way a new car company breaks in is by making a car that is so compelling that people are willing to pay extra for that car."

—

"In certain sectors, like automotive and solar and space, you don't see new entrants. There's not a lot of capital going to startups and not a lot of entrepreneurs going into those arenas. The problem is that in the absence of new entrants into an industry, you don't have that force of innovation. It's really new entrants that drive innovation more than anything.

That's why I have devoted my efforts to those industries, and they are industries that require quite a bit of capital to get going."

—

"What I actually tell the team is that everyone is the chief engineer. This is extremely important. Everyone must understand, broadly speaking, how all the systems in the vehicle work, so you don't have sub-system optimization because this is what naturally happens… The product errors reflect the organizational errors. Whatever departments you've got, that will be where your interfaces are and then instead of getting rid of something or questioning the constraints, the one department will design to the constraints that the other department has given them without calling into question those constraints and saying those constraints are wrong. You should actually take the approach that the constraints that you are given are guaranteed to be to some degree wrong… because the counterpoint to that would be that they are perfect… Question your constraints. It does not matter if the person handing you those constraints won a Nobel Prize; even Einstein was wrong some of the time."

—

"If you're going to try something innovative then you're in unexplored territory, so the odds that something will go wrong are pretty high. It's only if you try to do something that is well understood that there's little chance of failure."

—

"In terms of our competitiveness, it mostly comes down to our pace of innovation. Our pace of innovation is much, much faster than the big aerospace companies or the country-driven systems. This is generally true. If you look at innovation from large companies and from smaller companies, smaller companies are generally better at innovating than larger companies. It has to be that way from a Darwinian standpoint because smaller companies would just die if they didn't try innovating."

—

"When trying different things, you gotta have some acceptance of failure… Failure must be an option. If failure is not an option, it's going to result in extremely conservative choices and you may get something even worse than lack of innovation: things may go backwards."

—

"Just try weird stuff. It's nothing ventured, nothing gained. If we're too cautious, then how do we make revolutionary improvements? Revolutions are not done with caution. So, we want to try things, ideally things that don't break the whole system, but I think as long as we're agile and we react quickly to improve things and correct mistakes, I think it'll be fine."

—

"It is unfortunately common for many in academia to overweight the value of ideas and underweight bringing them to fruition. For example, the idea of going to the moon is trivial, but going to the moon is hard."

—

"Great things will never happen with VCs [venture capitalists] or professional managers. They have high drive, but they don't have the creativity or the insight. Some do, but most don't."

—

"Please note that Twitter will do lots of dumb things in coming months. We will keep what works and change what doesn't."

—

"The first controlled powered flight was 1903 with the Wright brothers. And then 66 years later, we put the first people on the moon. If you'd asked people, say, in 1900, 'What are the odds of man landing on the Moon?' they would have said, 'That's ridiculous.'"

—

"Too much respect for authority inhibits innovation."

—

"There needs to be an expectation of innovation, and the compensation structure must reflect that. There must also be an allowance for failure because if you are trying something new, necessarily there is some chance it will not work. If you punish people too much for failure, then they will respond accordingly, and the innovation you get will be very incrementalist. Nobody's going to try anything bold for fear of getting fired or being punished in some way. The risk-reward must be balanced and favor taking bold moves. Otherwise, it will not happen."

—

"Don't build moats, build tech trees."

—Elon Musk

APPLICATION:

Every once in a while, a company comes along that understands the nature of innovation. Because Tesla was not one of the first movers in the auto industry, they had to be unique. Not only did Tesla have to be different, but due to the deep establishment of the industry, they had to be VERY different. Today, a Tesla car not only blows all other electric vehicles out of the water, but also surpasses internal combustion engine cars. Tesla cars are highly regarded for their safety, performance, and advanced technology, namely autopilot. They're practically in a league of their own at this point, and competition is far from the minds of the great teams at Tesla. This attitude, which pervades the company, is initiated by Musk. He not only sets up an innovative culture at his companies but builds a compensation structure that promotes innovation:

"The massive thing that can be done is to make sure that your incentive structure is such that innovation is rewarded, and lack of innovation is punished. There's gotta be a carrot and a stick. So, if somebody is innovating and making good progress then they should be promoted sooner, and if somebody is completely failing to innovate—not every role requires innovation, but if they're in a role where innovation should be happening and it's not happening—they should either not be promoted or exited. Let me tell you, you'll get innovation real fast."

Not many companies go to these lengths to innovate, and they pay for it by taking their place behind Musk's companies (or at least behind those who take care to properly address the importance of innovation).

38. HORSE BLINDERS

PRINCIPLE:

DON'T SPREAD OUT YOUR FOCUS IF YOU WANT TO GO FAR.

The more you spread out your attention or focus, the more you decrease your ability to go far in one direction. Direct all of your energy and time primarily on a few dimensions in life, and you can make tremendous progress in those dimensions. Focus on what really matters.

QUOTES:

> "Focus is incredibly important. If you have a certain amount of resources, to the degree that you diffuse your focus, you impede your ability to execute."
>
> —

"We don't think too much about what competitors are doing because I think it's important to be focused on making the best possible products. It may be analogous to what they say about if you're in a race: 'Don't worry about what the other runners are doing—just run.'"

—

"Focus on signal over noise. A lot of companies get confused; they spend money on things that don't actually make the product better. For example, at Tesla, we've never spent any money on advertising. We put all the money into R&D and manufacturing and design to try to make the car as good as possible. I think that's the way to go. For any given company, keep thinking about 'Are these efforts that people are expending, are they resulting in a better product or service?' And if they're not, stop those efforts."

—

"Other companies spend money on advertising and manipulating public opinion, Tesla focuses on the product. I trust the people."

—

"The thing I really focus on at Tesla is really putting all of our money and attention into trying to make the product as compelling as possible, because

I think that really the way to sell any product is through word of mouth… the key is to have a product that people will love."

—

"Generally, people, if they're at a party or they're talking to friends or whatever, you'll talk about the things that you love, but if you just like something and it's OK, you're not going to care that much, but if you love something, you're gonna talk. Then that generates word of mouth, and that's basically how our sales have grown; we don't spend any money on advertising or endorsements. So, anyone who buys our car, they just bought it because they like the car, you know it's genuine… and no discounts, I actually pay full retail price for my own cars."

—

"If I ever do a tweet or a public announcement, it's got nothing to do with the stock price. What concerns me is I don't want customers thinking something that's wrong. For long-term investors in Tesla, the short-term fluctuations are not important. We cater actions in our announcements to the long-term investors in Tesla. Those are the ones we really care about. The people that are in it just to speculate and then are out the next day—we feel about them about the same way they feel about us: we don't care."

—Elon Musk

APPLICATION:

If you choose to focus on yourself or your organization, you can have the pleasure of being able to invite competition, as it poses no legitimate threat. Musk has always welcomed competition, even with Tesla and the cutthroat car industry: "We're very excited to see that the big car companies are embracing electric vehicles. If you were to rewind the press releases to five years ago that was not the case." And this is because: "When our competitors advertise for electric vehicles, every time they do that, our sales go up. It's pretty funny." Musk obsessively focuses on producing the highest-quality product possible to satisfy his customers. He always puts the quality of the product and the customer experience first. It's like he has horse blinders on, limiting his field of view to what matters the most.

This is not what most people do. Most entrepreneurs, out of fear, usually put a significant percentage of their mental energy toward their competitors. They try to analyze every little advantage or disadvantage they may have. Focusing on your competition is a self-fulfilling prophecy and a recipe for misery. The less you focus on your company, the less you will innovate, and as a result, you'll attract competition. Fundamentally, you will not go far; look at all the mediocre companies out there. They all have their focus spread out over unimportant matters.

Musk's ability to focus individually has been unbelievable from the very beginning. As a young boy, he often hyper-focused on something he was thinking about. People wouldn't be able to get through to him when he had a certain distant look in his eyes. This occurred so frequently that Musk's parents and doctors thought he might be deaf. They even had surgery performed to see if it would help, but there was no change. He still gets lost in thought to this day, and it's not due to a lack of focus, but rather an unusual ability to narrow his attention. Here is what Musk thinks is going on: "It seems as though the part of the brain that's usually reserved for visual processing—the part that is used to process images coming in from my eyes—gets taken over by internal thought processes." Musk continues: "I can't do this as much now because there are so many things demanding my attention but, as a kid, it happened a lot. That large part of your brain that's used to handle incoming images gets used for internal thinking." Musk conceives of this ability as analogous to a graphics chip in a computer. He can see things out in the real world, reproduce the image in his mind with clarity, and then imagine how those things could interact with each other: "For images and numbers, I can process their interrelationships and algorithmic relationships." Another man who had this ability was Nikola Tesla (according to his autobiography).

39. THE "BILLIONAIRE" THING

PRINCIPLE:

MONEY AMPLIFIES YOUR PERSONALITY;
IT DOESN'T DEFINE IT.

It doesn't make sense to hate on individuals simply for the fact
that they have amassed wealth, especially when they have done
so by inspiring people and making products that people love.
Hating on anyone is a waste of time.

QUOTES:

"For sure it would be very problematic if I were
consuming billions of dollars a year in personal consumption, but that's not the case. In fact, I don't
even own a home right now, I'm literally staying at
friends' places... I don't have a yacht, I really don't

take vacations. It's not as though my personal consumption is high… the one exception is a plane, but if I don't use the plane, I have less hours to work."

—

"I have a bunch of houses, but I don't spend a lot of time in most of them, and that doesn't seem like a good use of assets, like somebody could probably be enjoying those houses and get better use of them than me." [reason he sold his houses in 2020]

—

"Yeah, I'm back to spare bedroom/couch surfing at friends' houses in Silicon Valley, which I did for about a decade. Frankly, I like it this way, as I get to see my friends, who I love, more often." [2022]

—

"I think possessions kind of weigh you down, then they're kind of an attack vector."

—

"How does this wealth arise? If you organize people in a better way to produce products and services that are better than what existed before and you have some ownership in that company, then that essentially gives you the right to allocate more capital. There's a conflation of consumption and capital allocation."

—

"Ironically, the 'billionaire' label, when used by media, is almost always meant to devalue and denigrate the subject. I wasn't called that until my companies got to a certain size, but reality is that I still do the same science and engineering as before. Just the scale has changed."

—

"Use of the word 'billionaire' as a pejorative is morally wrong and dumb. If the reason for it is building products that make millions of people happy."

—

Interviewer (Barry Hurd): "Are you motivated beyond just profit motive and racking up dollars?"

Musk: "Yeah… I'm a volunteer. I don't need the money… It's not like I'm sitting here saying, 'I wish I could buy such and such a thing.' I could buy it. I get paid minimum wage actually, I don't even get paid overtime."

—

"The reason I am doing it [taking the risk of making electric cars] and certainly a lot of people at Tesla are doing it, is because we think it actually is going to make a difference in the world if we transition to sustainable transport sooner rather than later. We're not doing this because we thought it was a way to get rich."

—

"Long-term purpose of my Tesla stock is to help make life multi-planetary to ensure its continuance. The massive capital needs are in 10-20 years. By then, if we're fortunate, Tesla's goal of accelerating sustainable energy and autonomy will be mostly accomplished."

—

"I am accumulating resources to help make life multi-planetary and extend the light of consciousness to the stars."

—Elon Musk

APPLICATION:

Here's Musk's technical breakdown of the "billionaire" thing:

"I think there's a fundamental question of like, consumption vs capital allocation. This is probably going to get me into trouble but the paradigm of communism vs. capitalism is fundamentally orthogonal to the reality of actual economics in some ways. What you actually care about is the responsiveness of the feedback loops to maximize the happiness of the population. If more resources are controlled by entities that have poor response in their feedback loops, so if it's a monopoly corporation or a small oligopoly, or… a monopolistic corporation in the limit is the government. This is not to say that people that work at the government are bad—if those same people are put in a better operating system situation, the outcome would be much better. So, it's really just, what is the responsiveness of the organization to maximizing the happiness of the people? And so you want to have a competitive situation, where it's truly competitive and companies aren't gaming the system. And then where the rules are set correctly and you need to be on the alert for regulatory capture, where the referees are in fact captured by the players. The players should not control the referees."

The point Musk is making here is that those who are competent in capital allocation and maximizing the happiness of the population should be given the right to operate to the best of their abilities (within reason, of course; we don't want a bunch of monopolies). Because it has no competition, the government has little incentive to work hard and serve people optimally. If the government has no incentive to perform optimally, it doesn't make sense for them to be in control of everything.

Musk often works 16-hour days, 7 days a week, and either sleeps in the factory or a $50,000 house that SpaceX owns. He sold all his mansions and most of his material possessions. He believes they hinder his missions' progress. In an interview with Joe Rogan, Rogan asks: "What's a dream house for Elon Musk, like some Tony Stark type shit?"

Musk responds:

"Yeah, definitely. You gotta have the dome that opens up with the stealth helicopter... But then I was like, 'Man, does it really make sense for me to spend time designing and building a house...and I'd be real OCD on the little details and the design, or should I be allocating that time to getting us to Mars? I should probably do the latter [laughs]. You know, what's more important, Mars or a house? Mars.'"

We want an individual with this mindset to not be limited. We want these individuals to have plenty of access to resources!

40. THE FUTURE IS A BRANCHING SET OF PROBABILITIES

PRINCIPLE:

DIFFERENT ACTIONS WILL LEAD TO DIFFERENT FUTURES.

Think over the actions you could take and determine which ones matter the most to what you're trying to accomplish. Some actions matter far more to the outcome of your endeavor (and/or your life) than others.

QUOTES:

"The actions that we take change the probability that the future will be good."

—

"The future is a set of branching probability streams. Some actions by humanity have an extremely leveraged effect on shape and size of those streams."

—

"I look at the future from a standpoint of probabilities. It's like a branching stream of probabilities, and there are actions that we can take that affect those probabilities or that accelerate one thing or slow down another thing."

—

"I mean, you can really think of civilization as almost like a thermometer. Where you've got the red ball and then as the temperature rises the liquid expands and it goes up. And if you think about how civilization has really developed and we've put ourselves right on the edge of the water. If that water level rises even a little bit, you've got major problems. I think we need to think in terms that are not super binary. It's not like the future will definitely be good or the future will definitely be bad. This is just not the way it is. The actions that we take change the probability that the future will be good. It's not all or nothing. The sooner we transition to a sustainable energy future the better for the world. And I think it would be hard to find a reasonable person who would disagree with that."

—

"In general, critical thinking is good. Examining whether you have the correct axioms, are they the most applicable axioms? Does the logic necessarily connect? And then what are the range of probable outcomes? Outcomes are usually not deterministic, they're a range. So, you wanna figure out what those probabilities are and make sure ideally that you're the house. It's fine to gamble, as long as you're the house."

——

"The first step is to establish that something is possible; then probability will occur."

—Elon Musk

APPLICATION:

In many video games, some key decisions that you make early in the game affect the rest of the story. Real life isn't too different (maybe because life is a simulation too...?). Your actions can affect the probability that you (or other people) will experience some things rather than others, or that some events will occur in the world rather than others. It's one big decision tree with many branches, and each branch leads you to a subset of possible outcomes.

Musk was really into video games all throughout his childhood and teenage years. In college, thinking about what he wanted to dedicate his life to, he considered pursuing a career in video game design. But ultimately, he concluded that designing video games wouldn't be a grand enough pursuit: "It wouldn't have a big effect. Even though I have an intrinsic love of video games, I couldn't bring myself to do that as a career."

As you might imagine, this wasn't the only thing Musk had been pondering while at college. He used a scientific first-principles approach to narrow down five things that he thought were most essential to the future:

> "When I was in college, I just thought, what are the things that are most likely to affect the future of humanity at a macro level? It just seemed like it would be the internet, sustainable energy, making life multi-planetary, genetics, and AI The first three, if you worked on those, they were almost certainly going to be good, and the last two are a little more dodgy."

Looking back, we can see that he was serious about his ponderings, as he has made great strides in nearly all of these fields. These five items were Musk's real life video game φ story mode paths, and he has tried to take the set of actions that maximizes the accomplishment of his chosen goals over the decades.

φ A fun video game quote from Musk: "If life was a video game, the graphics are great, but the plot is confusing, and the tutorial is way too long." One video game Musk has recommended is *Elden Ring*.

41. ZOOMING OUT

PRINCIPLE:

BUILD A DEEP KNOWLEDGE LANDSCAPE
AND LOOK FOR CONNECTIONS.

When you collect information from many disciplines and culti-
vate general knowledge, you can zoom out and see connections
between things that others simply cannot see.

QUOTES:

"Most engineers don't feel strongly about politics
but do want to work with other great engineers.
Silicon Valley has world's best engineering talent,
but is co-located with San Francisco, which is far
left. Thus, far left gained control of an incredibly
powerful info weapon." [on Twitter]

—

"Music is a limbic resonator."

—

"Money, in my view, is essentially an information system for labor allocation, so it has no power in and of itself; it's like a database for guiding people as to what they should do."

—

"Let's just say that if something's flying over your head, there's a whole bunch of flying cars going all over the place, that is not an anxiety-reducing situation. You don't think to yourself, 'Well, I feel better about today.' You're thinking, 'Did they service their hubcap, or is it going to come off and guillotine me?' Things like that."

—

"Hardcore Democrats or Republicans never vote for the other side, so independent voters are the ones who actually decide who's in charge!"

—

"In your brain you have, I think, some intrinsic elements that represent beauty and that trigger the emotion of appreciation for beauty in your mind. And I think that these are actually relatively consistent among people. Not completely, not everyone likes the same thing, but there's a lot of commonality."

—

"A major part of real-world AI has to be solved to make unsupervised, generalized full self-driving work, as the entire road system is designed for biological neural nets with optical images."

—

"There was a shuttle tragedy [Space Shuttle Challenger, 1986] and seven people died and that's terrible, but a lot of people die all of the time... why do we care so much? Because it was the dream of exploration that was dying along with those people."

—

"Tesla is both a hardware and a software company, so a huge percentage of our engineers are actually software engineers, and you can think of our car as kind of like a laptop on wheels."

—

"A neuron doesn't realize it's a neuron."

—

"Recessions serve a vital economic cleansing function."

—

"It's really crazy that we build these sophisticated rockets and then crash them every time we fly. This is mad. So yeah, I can't emphasize how profound this is and how important reusability is. And often I'll be told: 'But you could get more payload if you made it expendable.' I said yes, you could also get more payload from an aircraft if you got rid of the landing gear and the flaps and just parachuted out when you got to your destination. But that would be crazy, and you would sell zero aircraft. So, reusability is absolutely fundamental."

—

"Existing franchise dealers have a fundamental conflict of interest between selling gasoline cars, which constitute the vast majority of their business, and selling the new technology of electric cars. It is impossible for them to explain the advantages of going electric without simultaneously undermining their traditional business. This would leave the electric car without a fair opportunity to make its case to an unfamiliar public."

—

"Every gasoline or diesel car that's going down the road has a de facto subsidy on it. People sometimes don't appreciate that. Whenever something is burning fossil fuels, it has a de facto subsidy. It's a subsidy of the public good. They're spending the carbon capacity of the oceans and atmosphere, not to mention the sulfur and nitrous oxide that are emitted, as it turns out, in greater quantities than regulators were told."

—

"There's a lot of people worried about life contamination [on Mars], but anything that can survive on Mars is so freaking tough, it's insane. It is cold and there's a lot of UV radiation, and it's not going to be too worried about anything we send from Earth."

—

"If you'd told somebody in '69 that we're not going to be back on the moon in like, 2020… you probably might even get punched, honestly… because it's so intolerably rude to the future."

—

"In the case of space flight, the critical breakthrough that's necessary in spaceflight is rapid and complete reusability of rockets, just as we have for aircraft. We can imagine that if an aircraft was single-use almost no one would fly. You can buy, say, a 747, it might be $250 million, $300 million, something like that—you'd need two of them for a round trip. Nobody's going to pay millions of dollars per ticket to fly... But because you can reuse the aircraft tens of thousands of times, air travel becomes much more affordable. The same is true of rockets."

—

"I think, frankly, it's probably a good thing that we do eventually die. You know, there's a saying in physics—even physicists, which are generally quite objective—there's a saying that all physicists don't change their mind, they just die. So, maybe, you know, it's good to have this life cycle."

—

"If we don't have sustainable energy generation, there's no way that we can conserve our way to a good future. We have to fundamentally make sustainable energy available."

—

"We already have a giant, free fusion reactor in the sky called the Sun. Just catch its energy with PV, store in battery and you're pretty much done." [on fusion power]

—

"It's quite surprising how little people know about geosciences, even pretty straightforward stuff like the carbon cycle. I mean, I've had conversations with quite smart and well-read people who don't understand that there is a surface carbon cycle, but if you dig stuff up from deep underground and add it to the surface carbon cycle, that fundamentally changes the chemical equilibrium of the surface of the Earth. And they're like, 'Wow, really?'"

—

"If we continue upon the Apollo program and get to Mars and beyond, that will seem far more important in historical context than anything else we do today. The day multi-planetary species come about, things like the Soviet Union will be forgotten or merely remembered by arcane historical scholars. Things like the invasion of Iraq won't even be a footnote."

—

"A gasoline tank has 10 times more combustion energy than our battery pack. Moreover, the Model S battery pack also has internal firewalls between the 16 modules and a firewall between the battery pack and passenger compartment. This effectively limits the fire energy to a few percent that of a gasoline car and is the reason why Dr. Shibayama was able to retrieve his pens and papers from the glove compartment completely untouched after the recent fire [caused by a high-speed impact with a tow hitch]. It is also why arsonists tend to favor gasoline. Trying to set the side of a building on fire with a battery pack is far less effective."

—

"I do worry about making sure that we can achieve affordability thresholds, because even if you make the value-for-money infinite, if people do not have enough money to buy it, then they still can't."

—

"I try to tell my team: 'Imagine there was a pallet of cash that was plummeting through the atmosphere, and it was going to burn up and smash into tiny pieces. Would you try to save it?' Probably yes. That sounds like a good idea." [rationale for trying to save and reuse their rocket]

—

"Probably in 10 years, more than a half of new vehicle production is electric in the United States… But if you were to, say, go out twenty years, overwhelmingly, things are electric and autonomous… There will not be a steering wheel [because of autonomy]… There will be people who have non-autonomous cars like people who have horses."

—

"In order to solve the sustainable energy question, we need sustainable energy production, which is going to come primarily in the form of solar—overwhelmingly in the form of solar, in my view. Then combine that with stationary storage and an electric vehicle, and you have a complete solution to a sustainable energy future. Those are the three parts that are needed, and those are the three things that I think Tesla should be providing."

—

"I think, actually, all modes of transport will become fully electric, with the ironic exception of rockets. There's just no way around Newton's third law."

—

"What SolarCity [now Tesla Solar] really is, is a giant distributed utility. And it's working in partnership with the house and the business and in competition with the big monopoly utility. I mean, I think it's literally power to the people."

—

"Fundamentally, if you don't have a compelling product at a compelling price, you don't have a great company."

—

"Some people have this absurd view that the economy is some magic horn of plenty, like it just makes stuff... Let me just break it to the fools out there: if you don't make stuff, there is no stuff."

—

"Science is discovering the essential truths about what exists in the universe, engineering is about creating things that never existed."

—

"What I thought, really, was that we'd lost the will to explore, that we lost the will to push the boundary, and in retrospect, that was actually a very foolish error. Because the United States is a nation of explorers. The United States is a distillation of the human spirit of exploration; it's ludicrous in retrospect to have made such an assumption.But people need to believe that it's possible and that it's not going to bankrupt them, they're not going to have to give up something important like health care. It's gotta be a cost that isn't going to meaningfully affect their standard of living."

—

"The most remarkable thing that we do have today is the internet and access to all the world's information from anywhere. Having a supercomputer in your pocket is, I think, something people wouldn't have predicted in *Back to the Future*."

—

"I was really into physics [as a young man] and I thought, well, we don't want to have civilization collapse if we run out of oil and that's the only way of getting around. And we're going to have to go back to horses. And we won't be able to maintain civilization. We could have mass starvation. Civilization would collapse. So, we've got to have electric cars."

—

"With the internet, anyone who had a connection anywhere in the world would have access to all the world's information, just like a nervous system. Humanity was effectively becoming a super organism and qualitatively different than what it had been before."

—

"I am a big believer in the market system. The market system is just the collective will of the people. That's all."

—

"The acid test for any two competing socioeconomic systems is which side needs to build a wall to keep people from escaping? That's the bad one!"

—

"Tesla is a vehicle for creating and producing many useful products."

—

"One square kilometer is a million square meters. And there's one kilowatt per square meter of solar energy. So, in one square kilometer, there is a gigawatt of solar energy… You could power the entire United States with about 150 to 200 square kilometers of solar panels. The entire United States. Take a corner of Utah. There's not much going on there. I've been there."

—

"I think AI is going to be incredibly sophisticated in 20 years. It seems to be accelerating. The tricky thing about predicting things when there is an exponential is that an exponential looks linear close up. But it's actually not linear. And AI appears to be accelerating, from what I can see."

—

"The lithium is actually 2% of the cell mass. It's like the salt in the salad. It's a very small amount of cell mass and a fairly small amount of the cost. It sounds like it's big because it's called lithium-ion, but our battery should be called nickel-graphite because it's mostly nickel and graphite."

—

"All of the battery packs for Tesla are currently recycled. There are recycling centers in North America and Europe and Asia. It kind of makes sense because you can just think of the battery packs as really high-quality ore. It's way better to mine a battery pack than rocks."

—

"Interesting to think of physics as a set of compression algorithms for the universe. That's basically what formulas are."

—

"It's called the Space 'Station,' but it's actually moving around Earth at ~25 times the speed of sound or ~10 times faster than a rifle bullet."

—

"A union is just another corporation. Far better for many companies to compete for your skills, so that you have maximum optionality."

—

"Brand is just a perception, and perception will match reality over time. Sometimes it will be ahead, other times it will be behind. But brand is simply a collective impression some have about a product."

—

"We are a pattern of ancient atoms."

—

"I think, certainly, we need to take a look at our immigration laws. If there are really talented people doing graduate courses and engineering at our universities, we really don't want to send them home. We want to try to do everything we can to keep them here. For every one person who's an ace engineer, there are probably 10 jobs that will be created if that person stays here. It's a huge multiplier effect."

—

"With our giant casting machines, we are literally trying to make full-size cars in the same way that toy cars are made."

—

"Nobody would suggest buying airplanes that only fly once and then crash into the ocean. That would be absurd…" [on rocket reusability]

—

"Tesla is technically a car like an iPhone is technically a phone."

—

"We're basically going to design a factory like you would design an advanced computer and, in fact, use engineers that are used to doing that and have them work on this. I found that once you sort of explain this to a first-rate engineer, the light bulb goes on and they're like, 'Wow.' As JB [Straubel] was saying, they spend huge amounts of effort trying to make a fraction of a percent of improvement on the product itself, but actually, that same amount of effort will yield an order of magnitude greater result if you focus on building the machine that builds the machine. A lot of engineers don't realize that this is possible, they think that there's a wall there. They're basically operating according to these invisible walls. So, we're in the process of just going through and explaining those walls don't exist."

—

"Something most people know, but don't realize they know, is that the world is almost entirely solar powered already. If the sun wasn't there, we'd be a frozen ice ball at 3 degrees Kelvin. The Sun powers the entire system of precipitation. The whole eco-system is solar powered."

—

"I think the reality of being president is that you're actually like a captain of a very huge ship that has a small rudder."

—

"Socialism vs. capitalism is not even the right question. What really matters is avoiding monopolies that restrict people's freedom."

—

"Money is just data that allows us to avoid the inconvenience of barter."

—

"Humans are absurdly concentrated on a tiny percentage of Earth's surface. That's why people in cities think Earth is 'full' of people, when in fact it is basically empty."

—

"The Golden State is cooking its golden geese." [2022, referring to California and Aesop's *The Goose that Laid the Golden Eggs*]

—

"In the future, we will look back—and by 'future,' I'm not talking about super far in the future—I'm talking about toward the end of the century—we will look back on gasoline-powered cars the same way we look back on coal: as a sort of quaint anachronism that's in a museum."

—

"As we go to a more autonomous future, the importance of entertainment and productivity [in cars] will become greater and greater. To the degree that if you're just sitting in your car and the car is fully autonomous and driving somewhere, the car is essentially your chauffeur."

—

"We should look at currencies from an information theory standpoint. Whichever has least error and latency will win."

—

"Words are a very lossy compression of thoughts."

—

"You can think of a corporation as like a cybernetic collective, that's far smarter than an individual."

—

"Because it consists of billions of bi-directional interactions per day, Twitter can be thought of as a collective, cybernetic super-intelligence."

—

"Owning a car that is not self-driving, in the long-term will be like owning a horse—you would own it and use it for sentimental reasons, but not for daily use."

—

"Realized what I have in common with environmentalists, but also why they're so annoyingly wrong: they are conservationists of what is, whereas they should be conservationists of our potential over time, our cosmic endowment." [Musk mentions that a friend pointed this out, but worth including here]

—

"What you've got going on with the internet is it's basically like an earthquake where the epicenter is Silicon Valley and it's shaking up the whole world." [1999]

—

"If the output is more valuable than the inputs… that's profit, the outputs are more valuable than the input. That says you have a useful company. In a high-growth scenario, you have a lot more inputs for future outputs, so you have negative cash flow and lack of profitability… In the long term of course, that has to be fixed. There can't be negative cash flow in the long term. There needs to be a net positive output, which is sort of profits, in the long term. But in the short-term, when there's high growth that isn't the most sensible thing."

—

"The profit motive is a good one if the rules of an industry are properly set up. So, there's nothing fundamentally wrong with profit. Profit just means that people are paying you more for whatever you're doing than you're spending to create it. That's a good thing. And if that's not the case, then you'll be out of business, and rightfully so because you're not adding enough value."

—

"When I was a little kid, I was really scared of the dark but then I came to understand dark just means the absence of photons in the visible wavelength, 400-700 nanometers. Then, I thought, 'Well, that's really silly to be afraid of a lack of photons' and then I wasn't afraid of the dark anymore after that."

—

"There are about 500M tweets per day and billions of impressions, so hate speech impressions are <0.1% of what's seen on Twitter!"

—

"The problem is that likes are public [on Twitter], subjecting people to criticism, and 'like' is often the wrong description, as you often just think something is interesting or notable, but not likable. We need to add these critical distinctions."

—

"It's a real problem [gatekeeping]. Apple and Google effectively control access to most of the internet via their app stores."

—

"I am neither conventionally right nor left, but I agree with your point. The woke mind virus has thoroughly penetrated entertainment and is pushing civilization towards suicide. There needs to be a counter-narrative."

—

"Truth over time builds trust. Nothing else."

—

"I can't think of a worse curse than living forever."

—

"Seems bizarre that it's so easy [to] enter illegally, but so hard to get a legal work visa." [in the US]

—

"The most entertaining outcome is the most likely— my variant on Occam's Razor." [Elon's Razor]

—

"App store fees are obviously too high due to the iOS/Android duopoly. It is a hidden 30% tax on the internet."

—

"The actual attackers in class-action lawsuits are the law firms. They just find someone in the class to be their puppet. Current class-action law is actually a massive tax on the American people and desperately needs reform. It is one of the reasons medication is so expensive in the USA. Somehow, other countries do just fine without class-action law."

—

"Twitter is like open-sourcing the news."

"Amphetamines negatively affect empathy; psychedelics do the opposite."

—

"At the end of the day, if Twitter is indeed the most accurate source of information, more people will use it."

—

"Widespread verification will democratize journalism and empower the voice of the people."

—

"How exciting to be alive at the same time as the largest animal ever! Wild that blue whales are bigger than the biggest dinosaur."

—

"Most probable outcome by far is a horrible war of attrition that destroys Ukraine and severely damages Russia, with massive body count on both sides. And, in the end, the same outcome. So why?"

—

"Russia has been punched in the nose and forced to retreat many times by Ukraine. But what you don't want to do is give Russia a choice of total, humiliating defeat or nukes—then the probability of them using nukes is high." [2022]

—

"But surely no reasonable person would launch nuclear war? The problem with that logic is if we were dealing with reasonable people, we wouldn't have war in the first place."

—

"There are no angels in war."

—

"War is the ultimate Supreme Court."

—

"Future wars are all about the drones. Human crews of planes or tanks have no chance. One exception: a purely analog, human-controlled vehicle is far more resilient to EMF weapons."

—

"Education is the path out of poverty and internet access enables education."

—

"Should be Alexander the Greatest. After all, is there a better Alexander?"

—

"Won't be long before we view gasoline cars the same way we view steam engines today."

—

"Ecosystem is almost entirely dependent on the sun already. Civilization's energy needs are absurdly tiny compared to what the sun sends us for free (~ 1 GWh/day/km^2)."

—

"Solar panels, ground mount, and rooftop, paired with stationary batteries, will be civilization's primary source of energy, as sure as day follows night. Mark these words."

—

"Fusion would be expensive energy, given difficulty of obtaining and transporting source fuel, plus maintaining the reactor. Far better to use the Sun—thermonuclear reactor with no need to refuel or service."

—

"The primary solution to a sustainable energy future is solar/wind with batteries for when sun doesn't shine or wind doesn't blow, interconnected with conventional high voltage lines. No unknown technology is needed! Hydro + geothermal + fission will also be non-trivial contributors."

—

"Countries should be increasing nuclear power generation! It is insane from a national security standpoint and bad for the environment to shut them down."

—

"Tesla is to protect life on Earth. SpaceX to extend life beyond."

—

"Speed for a rocket is always going to be roughly the same. The convenience and comfort is going to be about the same. Reliability has to be at least as good as what's been done before—otherwise, people won't use your rocket to launch multi-hundred-million-dollar satellites, but there's not going to be much improvement there. So, you're really left with one key parameter against which technology improvements must be judged, and that's cost."

—

"A platform cannot be considered inclusive or fair if it is biased against half the country." [on social media]

—

"Both the far left and far right have a lot of hate. One could simply replace the word 'far' with 'loathing,' as they have that emotion a lot, whereas most people, who are moderates, do not."

—

"70 is currently the age when you receive maximum Social Security benefits. In other words, that's when the government concludes that you can't hold a job!!"

—

"There are a couple of things that I think are pretty bogus. One is space mining, and another is space solar power. If you calculate how much it costs to bring either the photons from space solar power back to Earth or the raw material back to Earth, the economics don't make sense."

—

"You can only go there every two years because the orbital synchronization of Earth and Mars is about every two years… But I think it would be an interesting way for the civilization to develop. People would meet each other and be like, 'What orbital synchronization did you arrive on?'"

—

"Getting in a car will be like getting in an elevator—you just tell it where you want to go, and it takes you there with extreme levels of safety. That'll be normal."

—

"When people see who's investing in the IPO, it's the smartest, most long-term thinking investors in the market. It's really an amazing set of investors. So, I think it's just worth noting that the smartest money in the world is betting on Tesla. They must have a reason for doing so." [2010]

—

"People should never fear turbulence. Commercial airliner wings can handle insane amounts of bending."

—

"The duty of a leader is to serve their people, not for the people to serve them."

—

"If you don't push for radical breakthroughs, you're not going to get radical outcomes."

—

"What I find ironic about a lot of the naysayers is that they—the very same people—will transition from saying it was 'impossible' to saying it was 'obvious.' I am like, wait a second, was it obvious or impossible? It can't be both.'"

—Elon Musk

APPLICATION:

This is one of the most important principles in this book, hence the number of quotes.

Musk has several rare attributes, like his ability to visualize, think from first principles, capture the public's imagination, and inspire others. But one of his most powerful attributes is the ability to zoom out. He can look at things from a macro lens while most are stuck viewing things through a micro lens. Put another way, he can operate from the point of view of an eagle soaring above the land, scanning the terrain, while others are more like pheasants, stuck at ground level and only able to see what's right in front of them. He can see the forest, not just the trees. One of the largest contributing factors to this ability to zoom out is Musk's level of general awareness. When operating at a higher level of awareness, you can simply see what others cannot see.

An excellent example of when Musk's zooming-out ability was put on display was when he created The Boring Company. Musk would often be asked about what opportunities people should pursue and for a long time he would respond: "Can someone please start a tunneling company? Because I think tunnels have a lot of opportunity for alleviating traffic in cities and improving quality of life overall." Everyone thought Musk was joking, but eventually, he got so fed up with the traffic in L.A. that he tweeted: "Traffic is driving me nuts. Am going to build a tunnel boring machine and just start digging…" This tweet was put out on Dec. 17, 2016, and a month later they had a test dig site. They began digging in February 2017. Today the Boring Company has constructed a fully functioning tunnel in Las Vegas and is on its way to tackling "soul-destroying traffic." Although this undertaking seems to be a spontaneous thing, Musk had thought it through thoroughly:

> "The fundamental problem with cities is that we build cities in 3D. You've got these tall buildings with lots of people on each floor, but then you got roads, which are 2D. That obviously just doesn't work. You're guaranteed to have gridlock. But you can go 3D if you have tunnels. You are going to have many tunnels crisscrossing each other with maybe a few meters of vertical distance between them and completely get rid of traffic problems."

This is an exceptional insight—that transportation

networks and housing/living/working spaces need to have the same number of dimensions. If the dimensions of the two don't match, you have problems, like congestion/traffic. Through his vast accumulation of knowledge, specifically the tools of physics, Musk was able to zoom out, look at the fundamentals of the situation, and piece together a logical and more complete representation of the problem. Once he pieced together what was really going on, he could then move toward a solution relatively easily.

Of course, there are many forces at work when it comes to one's superior ability to see reality more clearly or from a different perspective, but a huge contributor to Musk's zooming-out capacity is that he simply has more knowledge in his head than the vast majority of people. The reason you have a more zoomed-out perception of the world as an adult, compared to when you were a kid, is that you've collected more information. People like Musk have simply collected even more useful information and are in the practice of forging connections within that knowledge base.

The more information you have in your head, the more connections you can make between those pieces of information, giving you a more complete map of the knowledge landscape.

42. THE MEANING OF LIFE

PRINCIPLE:

ORIENT YOUR EFFORTS TOWARD
ADVANCING CONSCIOUSNESS.

No one knows exactly what's going on. So, working towards
expanding Consciousness—and with it, our ability to ask the
right questions—is the only logical meaning of life for now.

QUOTES:

"I am inspired by curiosity. That is what drives me.
So let us expand the scope and scale of consciousness
so that we may aspire to understand the Universe."

—

"A new philosophy of the future is needed. I believe it should be curiosity about the Universe—expand humanity to become a multi-planet, then interstellar species to see what's out there."

—

"I hope consciousness propagates into the future and gets more sophisticated and complex and that it understands the questions to ask about the universe."

—

"I'm not trying to be some sort of savior or something like that... It seems like the obvious thing to do [working toward a better future for humanity], like I'm not sure why you would do anything else. You want to maximize the happiness of the population and propagate into the future as far as possible and understand the nature of reality. And from that, I think everything else follows."

—Elon Musk

APPLICATION:

Since the beginning of time, humanity has asked the question: 'Why are we here?' We have come up with many answers over the years. However, the most rational answer to this question is hardly mentioned or discussed. Continue reading for Musk's overall philosophy on life.

As mentioned earlier, Musk did not have a pleasant childhood. It was miserable much of the time. According to Musk, he'd go to school, get bullied, and then come home and be psychologically tortured by his father. In life, when you hit certain levels of pain, you go into a truth-seeking mode, doing everything you can to find meaning to guard against suffering. Humans have an unbelievable ability to march onward against horrific circumstances as long as we have meaning in our core. In his early teen years, Musk searched everywhere for meaning. He read numerous religious and philosophical texts. None of the ideologies resonated until he came across Douglas Adams' *The Hitchhiker's Guide to the Galaxy*:

> "When I was a teenager, I had an existential crisis trying to figure out, what's the meaning of life...There doesn't seem to be any meaning... for me at least the religious texts and I read all of them that I could get my hands on, did not seem convincing... Then I started reading the philosophers. Be careful of reading German philosophers as a teenager, it's not going to help with your depression [laughs]. Reading Schopenhauer and Nietzsche [he grimaces] ... as an adult, it's much more manageable, but as a kid you're like, 'Woah.' So, then I was like, 'Man, I'm struggling to find meaning in life here' and then I read *The Hitchhiker's Guide to the Galaxy* and basically what Douglas Adams was saying was that we don't really know what the right questions are to ask, like the question is not 'What's the meaning of life?'... In *The Hitchhiker's Guide to the Galaxy* [SPOILER], Earth, it turns out, is a big

computer and its goal is to answer the question, what's the meaning of life? And Earth comes up with the answer 42… In that book, which is really sort of an… existential philosophy book disguised as humor, they come to the conclusion that the real problem is trying to formulate the question… One way of characterizing this is to say, the universe is the answer, what is the question, or what are the questions? The more we can expand the scope and scale of consciousness, the better we can understand what questions to ask about the answer that is the universe. And the more we can expand consciousness and become a multi-planetary species and ultimately a multi-stellar species, we have a chance at figuring out what the hell is going on. This is why I think we should have more humans and more both biological and digital consciousness, and why we should become a multi-planet species and a multi-stellar species… is so that we can understand the nature of the universe. And then in order for that to occur, we have to make sure that things are good on Earth… so sustainable energy is important for ensuring the long-term viability of Earth and making life multi-planetary is important for extending consciousness."

Douglas Adams ✥ is an underrated philosopher.

✥ Hopefully it's obvious by now, but this book's title is partly inspired by Douglas Adams' *The Hitchhiker's Guide to the Galaxy* and of course Musk's connection to the book. Check out the original!

3 ESSENTIAL PRINCIPLES

If you remember anything from this book, I suggest these three principles:

RUN AND OPTIMIZE A FEEDBACK LOOP IN YOUR MIND: Gather experiences and information, collect people's input, think it over, and take action to improve your output. This may mean changing an existing behavior. Repeat.

JUST TAKE ACTION: Be careful not to overthink everything in an unconscious effort to avoid taking action. Take the first step and just start. You will never be 100% ready, and those who simply start will pass all those who hesitate, even if things are not perfect. You know deep down that simply taking action is what you need to do, so do it.

PUT IN THE WORK: What you put in is what you get out. Work hard across the board. Every single successful individual has taken advantage of compounding by simply putting in more time and energy than most.

ENDNOTES

ELON MUSK BOOK RECOMMENDATIONS

This section has been included because many of us today wish we knew which books the great people of the past valued. Someone in the future (or now) will appreciate this list. Obviously, it's not Musk's full lifetime reading list, but instead a list of books that he has recommended or praised over the years.

- *Benjamin Franklin: An American Life* by Walter Isaacson
- *Catherine the Great: Portrait of a Woman* by Robert K. Massie
- *Daemon* by Daniel Suarez
- *Dune* by Frank Herbert
- *Encyclopedia Britannica* (haha)
- *Foundation series* by Isaac Asimov
- *Game of Thrones* by George R. R. Martin
- *Human Compatible* by Stuart Russell
- *Ignition* by John Clarke
- *Life 3.0* by Max Tegmark
- *Liftoff* by Eric Berger
- *Lying* by Sam Harris
- *Masters of Doom* by David Kushner

- *Merchants of Doubt* by Erik M. Conway and Naomi Oreskes
- *Modern Engineering for Design of Liquid Propellant Rocket Engines* by Dieter K. Huzel, David H. Huang
- *On Writing* by Stephen King
- *Our Final Invention* by James Barrat
- *Player of Games, Excession, Surface Detail, Look to Windward* by Iain Banks
- *Steve Jobs* by Walter Isaacson
- *Storm of Steel* by Ernst Jünger
- *Story of Civilization* by Will and Ariel Durant
- *Superintelligence* by Nick Bostrom
- *The Big Picture: On the Origins of Life, Meaning, & the Universe Itself* by Sean Carroll
- *The Fault in Our Stars* by John Green
- *The Hitchhiker's Guide to the Galaxy* by Douglas Adams
- *The Lord of the Rings* by J.R.R. Tolkien
- *The Lost Planet* by Rachel Searles
- *The Machine Stops* by E. M. Forster
- *The Moon is a Harsh Mistress* by Robert A. Heinlein
- *The Skeptic's Guide to the Universe* by Dr. Steven Novella
- *Wages of Destruction* by Adam Tooze
- *What's Our Problem?* by Tim Urban
- *What We Owe the Future* by William MaCaskill
- *Wealth of Nations* by Adam Smith

FINAL WORD FROM THE AUTHOR

Well, I hope there's a good chance your mind has been altered after reading the words in this book. Mine certainly was after listening to Musk over the years, and even more so when I put this together. I encourage you to take the information in this book very seriously. We as humans have so much potential, and we are destined for great things… but the days of prosperity only come when we apply ourselves. We must educate one another, raise our levels of Consciousness and actualize our potential. So much time and energy is wasted on trivial nonsense today—there are grander things that desperately require our individual and collective attention. Think about how much excitement we have before us: walking on the sands of Mars, AI freeing us of miserable life experiences such as dangerous and damaging manual labor, the cures for all diseases, uncovering the mysteries of the past (check out Graham Hancock and Randall Carlson), and yes, eventually world peace. These things are all within Mankind's potential, but it's the actions that we take today that will determine whether we make it to those futures. I am devoting my life to helping make these things happen, and I hope you will too.

Finally, I would like to give thanks to all those who made

this book possible. Writing this book was one of my favorite experiences in this life so far.

Thank you, Elon Musk.

Thank you: Ellen Fishbein, Brian Meeks, Steve Jurvetson, Yoanna Stefanova, Perry Lambson, Mishael Edegwa, Johnna Crider, Gail Alfar, Wally Simon, Teri Ambrose, Davis Smith, Robin Erickson, Bridger Wenzel, Russell Smith, and the Musk University followers!

SOURCES

COOL INTRO QUOTE

1. Twitter, https://twitter.com/elonmusk/status/1531058755353419784?s=20&t=KF7VeRnELYAzvM573Z9I6g. Accessed 16 Jan. 2023.

OVERVIEW OF ELON MUSK

1. Vance, Ashlee. Elon Musk. Ecco, 2015.
2. Elon Musk on the Early Days of Tesla: Interview Part 1. YouTube, https://www.youtube.com/watch?v=AeeeEDSekG8. Accessed 18 Apr. 2023.
3. "What Is OpenAI? Definition and History from TechTarget." Enterprise AI, https://www.techtarget.com/searchenterpriseai/definition/OpenAI. Accessed 18 Apr. 2023.
4. Alvarez, Simon. "Neuralink Shares Video of Monkey Telepathically 'Typing' Using Keyboard." TESLARATI, 1 Dec. 2022, https://www.teslarati.com/neuralink-monkey-telepathic-typing-virtual-keyboard-demo-video/.

5. Merano, Maria. "The Boring Company Vegas Loop to Double in Size." TESLARATI, 22 Mar. 2023, https://www.teslarati.com/the-boring-company-vegas-loop-65-miles/.
6. Alvarez, Simon. "Elon Musk: Twitter Could Hit
7. over 1 Billion Monthly Users in 1-1.5 Years." TESLARATI, 27 Nov. 2022, https://www.teslarati.com/elon-musk-twitter-over-1-billion-monthly-users-2-years/.

FEEDBACK LOOPS

1. Schwantes, Marcel. "Elon Musk Shows How to Be a Great Leader with What He Calls His 'Single Best Piece of Advice.'" Inc.com, 12 July 2018, https://www.inc.com/marcel-schwantes/elon-musk-shows-how-to-be-a-great-leader-with-what-he-calls-his-single-best-piece-of-advice.html.
2. World Government Summit. Mohammad Al Gergawi in a Conversation with Elon Musk during WGS17. YouTube, 15 Feb. 2017, https://www.youtube.com/watch?v=rCoFKUJ_8Yo.
3. Engineering Physics Project Lab. What Elon Musk Says about Negative Feedback. YouTube, 31 Mar. 2014, https://www.youtube.com/watch?v=R3iagXcrjzU.
4. ---. What Elon Musk Says about Negative Feedback. YouTube, 31 Mar. 2014, https://www.youtube.com/watch?v=R3iagXcrjzU.

5. Condé Nast. "Watch Elon Musk and Y Combinator President on Thinking for the Future - FULL CONVERSATION | The New Establishment | Vanity Fair." Vanity Fair, 8 Oct. 2015, https://www.vanityfair.com/video/watch/elon-musk-y-combinator-president-thinking-for-the-future

6. Elon Musk: Elon Musk's Vision for the Future [Entire Talk]. YouTube, https://www.youtube.com/watch?v=SVk1hb0ZOrE. Accessed 21 Apr. 2023.

7. Export-Import Bank of the United States. 2014 Annual Conference| Discussion with Elon Musk. YouTube, 3 July 2017, https://www.youtube.com/watch?v=5ImZX-TRyszE.

8. Twitter, https://twitter.com/MuskUniversity/status/1559599274777665536. Accessed 21 Apr. 2023.

9. Elon Musk Videos Viral. Elon Musk on How To Start A Business. YouTube, 5 Nov. 2017, https://www.youtube.com/watch?v=1RyuQR4qUgs.

10. Twitter, https://twitter.com/elonmusk/status/1590383937284870145?s=20. Accessed 21 Apr. 2023.

TAKE ACTION

1. Elon Musk: A Future Worth Getting Excited about | TED | Tesla Texas Gigafactory Interview. YouTube, 18 Apr. 2022, https://www.youtube.com/watch?v=YRvf-00NooN8.

2. Outcast Motivation. MIND BLOWING WORK ETHIC - Elon Musk Motivational Video. YouTube, 14 Nov. 2021, https://www.youtube.com/watch?v=-U5d-EdWouDY.

3. Stanford eCorner. Elon Musk: Elon Musk's Vision for the Future [Entire Talk]. YouTube, 11 Dec. 2015, https://www.youtube.com/watch?v=SVk1hb0ZOrE.

4. Anderson, Chris. "Elon Musk's Mission to Mars | WIRED." WIRED, WIRED, 21 Oct. 2012, https://www.wired.com/2012/10/ff-elon-musk-qa/.

5. Twitter, https://twitter.com/elonmusk/status/1590383937284870145. Accessed 17 Jan. 2023.

6. Motive. Elon Musk - Challenge And How He Scaled Through. YouTube, 13 Nov. 2020, https://www.youtube.com/watch?v=gXjllXe66iQ.

FIRST PRINCIPLES

1. Lex Clips. How Elon Musk Solves Problems: First Principles Thinking Explained | Lex Fridman Podcast Clips. YouTube, 31 Dec. 2021, https://www.youtube.com/watch?v=54OSbbtXrdI.

2. Elon Musk USC Commencement Speech | USC Marshall School of Business Undergraduate Commencement 2014. YouTube, 17 May 2014, https://www.youtube.com/watch?v=e7Qh-vwpYH8.

3. Beach Bali Channel. Elon Musk with Nadiem Makarim Full Live Interview at Kampus Merdeka Festival | G20 Indonesia 2022. YouTube, 14 Nov. 2022, https://www.youtube.com/watch?v=Xp-fZcMOsdw.

4. Ohnsman, Alan. "A New Henry Ford: Elon Musk and His Model S | The Independent | The Independent." The Independent, The Independent, 17 July 2013, https://www.independent.co.uk/news/business/analysis-and-features/a-new-henry-ford-elon-musk-and-his-model-s-8715284.html.

5. Elon Musk Answers Your Questions! | SXSW 2018. YouTube, 12 Mar. 2018, https://www.youtube.com/watch?v=kzlUyrccbos

6. Anderson, Chris. "Elon Musk's Mission to Mars | WIRED." WIRED, WIRED, 21 Oct. 2012, https://www.wired.com/2012/10/ff-elon-musk-qa/.

7. "I Am Elon Musk, CEO/CTO of a Rocket Company, AMA! : IAmA." Reddit, https://www.reddit.com/r/IAmA/comments/2rgsan/i_am_elon_musk_ceocto_of_a_rocket_company_ama/. Accessed 16 Jan. 2023.

8. Innomind. The First Principles Method Explained by Elon Musk. YouTube, 4 Dec. 2013, https://www.youtube.com/watch?v=NV3sBlRgzTI.

SCHOOL ≠ EDUCATION

1. Elon Musk Videos Viral. Elon Musk "I Don't Give A Damn About Your Degree." YouTube, 10 Feb. 2018, https://www.youtube.com/watch?v=CQbKctnnA-Y.

2. Politics, Space Policy. Elon Musk, Satellite 2020 Conference, Washington DC, March 9, 2020. YouTube, 24 Mar. 2020, https://www.youtube.com/watch?v=ywPqLCc9zBU

3. Elon Musk | SXSW Live 2013 | SXSW ON. YouTube, 10 Mar. 2015, https://www.youtube.com/watch?v=Le-QMWdOMa-A.

4. Fisbeck, Hagen. Elon Musk: AxelSpringer Award Talk with Questions from Other CEOs - 1.12.2020. YouTube, 1 Dec. 2020, https://www.youtube.com/watch?v=heH1pWSqHN0.

5. shazmosushi. Elon Musk's 2003 Stanford University Entrepreneurial Thought Leaders Lecture. YouTube, 12 July 2013, https://www.youtube.com/watch?v=afZ-TrfvB2AQ.

6. Everyday Astronaut. A Conversation with Elon Musk about Starship. YouTube, 1 Oct. 2019, https://www.youtube.com/watch?v=cIQ36Kt7UVg.

7. Politics, Space Policy. Elon Musk, Satellite 2020 Conference, Washington DC, March 9, 2020. YouTube, 24 Mar. 2020, https://www.youtube.com/watch?v=ywPqLCc9zBU.

8. Endelman, Judith. "Collecting Innovation Today." Thehenryford.Org, The Henry Ford, 26 June 2008, https://www.thehenryford.org/documents/default-source/default-document-library/transcript_musk_full-length.pdf?sfvrsn=f5722f01_0.

9. Elon Musk Videos. Elon Musk and Bill Gates Discuss A.I., Entrepreneurship and More 2015. YouTube, 25 Nov. 2015, https://www.youtube.com/watch?v=OLi0seDZoaI.

10. "EDUCATION Should Be like VIDEO GAMES - Elon Musk #shorts - YouTube." YouTube, 9 Feb. 2022, https://www.youtube.com/shorts/d1VZtQUinoQ.

11. Elon Musk | SXSW Live 2013 | SXSW ON. YouTube, 10 Mar. 2015, https://www.youtube.com/watch?v=Le-QMWdOMa-A.

12. Elon Alerts. Elon Musk Interviewed by Indonesian Education Minister—14 November 2022. YouTube, 15 Nov. 2022, https://www.youtube.com/watch?v=l8sM-FMBfFrM.

GET IT DONE, OR DIE TRYING

1. ditschiu. Elon Musk- Never Give Up. YouTube, 24 Mar. 2018, https://www.youtube.com/watch?v=bheHjqvkaaI.
2. Lex Clips. Elon Musk: F*ck That, We'll Get It Done | Lex Fridman Podcast Clips. YouTube, 28 Dec. 2021, https://www.youtube.com/watch?v=KoihlAl7ugQ.
3. TriosMediaVids. Elon Musk Interview. YouTube, 11 Aug. 2012, https://www.youtube.com/watch?v=QLK_oIEJ860.
4. Motive. Elon Musk - Challenge And How He Scaled Through. YouTube, 13 Nov. 2020, https://www.youtube.com/watch?v=gXjllXe66iQ.
5. Hoffman, Carl. "Now 0-for-3, SpaceX's Elon Musk Vows to Make Orbit | WIRED." WIRED, WIRED, 5 Aug. 2008, https://www.wired.com/2008/08/musk-qa/.
6. Forum - International Business. Clean Tech Summit 2011 - IPO Spotlight with Elon Musk. YouTube, 3 Feb. 2011, https://www.youtube.com/watch?v=hTB-ZGWEzR_E.
7. PandoDaily. PandoMonthly: Fireside Chat With Elon Musk. YouTube, 17 July 2012, https://www.youtube.com/watch?v=uegOUmgKB4E.
8. Motive. Elon Musk - Challenge And How He Scaled Through. YouTube, 13 Nov. 2020, https://www.youtube.com/watch?v=gXjllXe66iQ.
9. Twitter, https://twitter.com/elonmusk/status/1532265043391291392?s=20&t=iw-MdsDUIYhcmY5I02vuaA. Accessed 16 Jan. 2023.

10. Swisher, Kara. "Elon Musk: 'A.I. Doesn't Need to Hate Us to Destroy Us.'" www.nytimes.com, Sway, 28 Sept. 2020, https://www.nytimes.com/2020/09/28/opinion/sway-kara-swisher-elon-musk.html.

11. Elon Musk Talks Twitter, Tesla and How His Brain Works — Live at TED2022. YouTube, 14 Apr. 2022, https://www.youtube.com/watch?v=cdZZpaB2kDM.

12. Outcast Motivation. SPINE-CHILLING WORK ETHIC - Elon Musk Motivational Speech Video (MUST WATCH!). YouTube, 30 May 2021, https://www.youtube.com/watch?v=hmlvr0_FBHM.

13. Davenport, Christian. The Space Barons. PublicAffairs, 2019.

14. Twitter, https://twitter.com/elonmusk/status/15828055 23484680192?s=20&t=iw-MdsDUIYhcmY5I02vuaA. Accessed 16 Jan. 2023.

15. Vance, Ashlee. Elon Musk. Ecco, 2015.

CAREERS AND PASSIONS

1. Motive. Elon Musk - Challenge And How He Scaled Through. YouTube, 13 Nov. 2020, https://www.youtube.com/watch?v=gXjllXe66iQ.

2. Harris, Paul. "Elon Musk: 'I'm Planning to Retire to Mars' | Elon Musk | The Guardian." The Guardian, The Guardian, 31 July 2010, https://www.theguardian.com/technology/2010/aug/01/elon-musk-spacex-rocket-mars.

3. "The Next, Next Thing—The Pennsylvania Gazette." The Pennsylvania Gazette, 1 Nov. 2008, https://thepenngazette.com/the-next-next-thing/.

4. SameerKDV. Full Speech of Elon Musk IAC 2017. YouTube, 29 Sept. 2017, https://www.youtube.com/watch?v=wM5D_SPBIv8.

5. Twitter, https://twitter.com/elonmusk/status/10124165 42724665346?s=20&t=iw-MdsDUIYhcmY5I02vuaA. Accessed 16 Jan. 2023.

6. HD Elon Musk's Inspiring Speech at SXSW 2018. YouTube, 18 Mar. 2018, https://www.youtube.com/watch?v=iW9Mwrb0XRg.

CONFORMITY = DEATH OF POTENTIAL

1. MulliganBrothers. Elon Musk Incredible Speech - Motivational Video 2017. YouTube, 29 Oct. 2017, https://www.youtube.com/watch?v=wD3pflBggMQ.

2. Elon Musk Reveals His Knowledge on Aliens, Challenges Putin to UFC, and Predicts WW3. YouTube, 5 Aug. 2022, https://www.youtube.com/watch?v=fXS_gkWAIs0.

3. Elon Musk Answers Your Questions! | SXSW 2018. YouTube, 12 Mar. 2018, https://www.youtube.com/watch?v=kzlUyrccbos.

4. The Space Archive. RAW Elon Musk Interview from Air Warfare Symposium 2020. YouTube, 2 Mar. 2020, https://www.youtube.com/watch?v=sp8smJFaKYE.

5. Twitter, https://twitter.com/elonmusk/status/15598234 34028400640?s=20&t=iw-MdsDUIYhcmY5I02vuaA. Accessed 16 Jan. 2023.

6. Elon and Kimbal Musk Interview. YouTube, 7 Jan. 2014, https://www.youtube.com/watch?v=1u6kQIzza-PI.

7. New Elon Musk Interview From World Government Summit 2023 with Timestamps. YouTube, https://www.youtube.com/watch?v=vrz5IOIGkBg. Accessed 15 Feb. 2023.

8. "The Tesla Approach to Distributing and Servicing Cars | Tesla." Tesla, https://www.tesla.com/blog/tesla-approach-distributing-and-servicing-cars. Accessed 16 Jan. 2023.

9. Vance, Ashlee. Elon Musk. Ecco, 2015.

10. Daum, Meghan. "Elon Musk, CEO of Tesla and SpaceX, Wants to Change How (and Where) Humans Live | Vogue." Vogue, Vogue, 21 Sept. 2015, https://www.vogue.com/article/elon-musk-profile-entrepreneur-spacex-tesla-motors.

11. Twitter, https://twitter.com/elonmusk/status/15200158 59162488835?s=20&t=iw-MdsDUIYhcmY5I02vuaA. Accessed 16 Jan. 2023.

EVOLUTION AND THE WORLD TODAY

1. PowerfulJRE. Joe Rogan Experience #1169 - Elon Musk. YouTube, 7 Sept. 2018, https://www.youtube.com/watch?v=ycPr5-27vSI.

2. Twitter, https://twitter.com/elonmusk/status/1494400631712501764?s=20&t=KF7VeRnELYAzvM573Z9I6g. Accessed 16 Jan. 2023.

3. Twitter, https://twitter.com/elonmusk/status/1524788481477816324?s=20&t=KF7VeRnELYAzvM573Z9I6g. Accessed 16 Jan. 2023.

4. Twitter, https://twitter.com/elonmusk/status/1531499523268575232?s=20&t=KF7VeRnELYAzvM573Z9I6g. Accessed 16 Jan. 2023.

5. Twitter, https://twitter.com/elonmusk/status/15050223 19915421696?s=20&t=dWAQxXM2kSrTuSxmnJ5JaA. Accessed 16 Jan. 2023.

6. Twitter, https://twitter.com/elonmusk/status/1576638490330116101?s=20&t=GOryLV-3QsmBuN_eTv8fMQ. Accessed 16 Jan. 2023.

7. Elon Musk: Neuralink, AI, Autopilot, and the Pale Blue Dot | Lex Fridman Podcast #49. YouTube, https://www.youtube.com/watch?v=smK9dgdTl40. Accessed 21 Apr. 2023.

8. Twitter, https://twitter.com/elonmusk/status/1559690651687608321?s=20&t=KF7VeRnELYAzvM573Z9I6g. Accessed 21 Apr. 2023.

9. Twitter, https://twitter.com/elonmusk/status/1589993413973544960?s=20&t=KF7VeRnELYAzvM573Z9I6g. Accessed 21 Apr. 2023.

10. Twitter, https://twitter.com/elonmusk/status/1589639376186724354?s=20&t=KF7VeRnELYAzvM573Z9I6g. Accessed 21 Apr. 2023.

11. Twitter, https://twitter.com/elonmusk/status/1598718904830132225?s=20. Accessed 21 Apr. 2023.

12. Twitter, https://twitter.com/elonmusk/status/1596942103937921025?s=20. Accessed 21 Apr. 2023.

LEADING FROM THE FRONT

1. Elon Musk Talks Twitter, Tesla and How His Brain Works — Live at TED2022. YouTube, https://www.youtube.com/watch?v=cdZZpaB2kDM. Accessed 21 Apr. 2023.

2. Twitter, https://twitter.com/teslaownersSV/status/1583557355408486400. Accessed 16 Jan. 2023.

3. Stock Market Insights | Seeking Alpha. https://seekingalpha.com/article/3971543-tesla-motors-tsla-elon-reeve-musk-on-q1-2016-results-earnings-call-transcript. Accessed 21 Apr. 2023.

4. Twitter, https://twitter.com/elonmusk/status/156474730364646265346?s=20&t=iw-MdsDUIYhcmY5I02vuaA. Accessed 16 Jan. 2023.

5. Twitter, https://twitter.com/elonmusk/status/1522918526520070144?s=20&t=JDx22txj_QiFtQmTiP-KeA. Accessed 16 Jan. 2023.

6. Intelligence, Tesla. Full New Elon Musk Interview. Ron Baron Conference Nov 2022. With Timestamps. YouTube, 4 Nov. 2022, https://www.youtube.com/watch?v=P7wUNMyK3Gs

7. Vance, Ashlee. Elon Musk. Ecco, 2015.

PROACTIVE VS. REACTIVE

1. Brandalise, Caleb. Elon Musk - Full Interview : July 15, 2017 NGA Conference. YouTube, 16 July 2017, https://www.youtube.com/watch?v=PeKqlDURpf8.

2. Swisher, Kara. "Elon Musk: 'A.I. Doesn't Need to Hate Us to Destroy Us.'" www.nytimes.com, Sway, 28 Sept. 2020, https://www.nytimes.com/2020/09/28/opinion/sway-kara-swisher-elon-musk.html.

3. Place - Energy Meeting. Elon Musk, CEO of Tesla at ONS 2014. YouTube, 13 Nov. 2014, https://www.youtube.com/watch?v=0ZsVxSDB7NY.

4. Hoffman, Carl. "Elon Musk, the Rocket Man With a Sweet Ride | Science| Smithsonian Magazine." Smithsonian Magazine, Smithsonian Magazine, 1 Dec. 2012, https://www.smithsonianmag.com/science-nature/elon-musk-the-rocket-man-with-a-sweet-ride-136059680/.

5. Computer History Museum. CHM Revolutionaries: An Evening with Elon Musk. YouTube, 18 Mar. 2013, https://www.youtube.com/watch?v=A5FMY-K-o0Q.

6. Place - Energy Meeting. Elon Musk, CEO of Tesla at ONS 2014. YouTube, 13 Nov. 2014, https://www.youtube.com/watch?v=0ZsVxSDB7NY.

7. Hoffman, Carl. "Elon Musk, the Rocket Man With a Sweet Ride | Science| Smithsonian Magazine." Smithsonian Magazine, 1 Dec. 2012, https://www.smithsonianmag.com/science-nature/elon-musk-the-rocket-man-with-a-sweet-ride-136059680/.

8. Computer History Museum. CHM Revolutionaries: An Evening with Elon Musk. YouTube, 18 Mar. 2013, https://www.youtube.com/watch?v=A5FMY-K-o0Q.

9. Place - Energy Meeting. Elon Musk, CEO of Tesla at ONS 2014. YouTube, 13 Nov. 2014, https://www.youtube.com/watch?v=0ZsVxSDB7NY.

10. Davis, Johnny. "One More Giant Leap." The Telegraph, The Telegraph, 4AD, https://www.telegraph.co.uk/culture/3666994/One-more-giant-leap.html.

11. Université Paris 1 Panthéon-Sorbonne. Conversation avec Elon Musk à Paris 1 Panthéon-Sorbonne. YouTube, 3 Dec. 2015, https://www.youtube.com/watch?v=BMskI6G9ty0.

12. Université Paris 1 Panthéon-Sorbonne. Conversation avec Elon Musk à Paris 1 Panthéon-Sorbonne. YouTube, 3 Dec. 2015, https://www.youtube.com/watch?v=BMskI6G9ty0.

13. Videos, All Elon Musk. Elon Musk About Mars & Renewable Energy at AGU - 2015. YouTube, 12 Sept. 2016, https://www.youtube.com/watch?v=h7hoCfEaUsQ.

14. Twitter, https://twitter.com/elonmusk/status/15334107 45429413888?s=20&t=iw-MdsDUIYhcmY5I02vuaA. Accessed 16 Jan. 2023.

15. PowerfulJRE. Joe Rogan Experience #1169 - Elon Musk. YouTube, 7 Sept. 2018, https://www.youtube. com/watch?v=ycPr5-27vSI.

16. Elon Musk: A Future Worth Getting Excited about | TED | Tesla Texas Gigafactory Interview. YouTube, https://www.youtube.com/watch?v=YRvf00NooN8. Accessed 21 Apr. 2023.

17. Twitter, https://twitter.com/elonmusk/status/1281121339584114691?s=20. Accessed 21 Apr. 2023.

IMPORTANCE OF PASSING THE GREAT FILTERS

1. Twitter, https://twitter.com/elonmusk/status/14635622 89643151360?s=20&t=iw-MdsDUIYhcmY5I02vuaA. Accessed 16 Jan. 2023.

2. O'Neill, Natalie. "Elon Musk's SpaceX Colony on Mars Won't Follow Earth-Based Laws." New York Post, 30 Oct. 2020, https://nypost.com/2020/10/30/elon-musks-spacex-colony-on-mars-wont-follow-earth-based-laws/.

3. Endelman, Judith. "Collecting Innovation Today." The Henry Ford, 26 June 2008, https://www.thehenryford. org/documents/default-source/default-document-library/transcript_musk_full-length.pdf?sfvrsn=f5722f01_0.

4. Online Harbour. WAIC 2019 - Elon Musk and Jack Ma - Artificial Intelligence Debate. YouTube, 2 Sept. 2019, https://www.youtube.com/watch?v=Vpx-2F6L8ST4.

5. Twitter, https://twitter.com/elonmusk/status/12562542 91758551041?s=20&t=iw-MdsDUIYhcmY5I02vuaA. Accessed 16 Jan. 2023.

6. Twitter, https://twitter.com/elonmusk/status/15295610 71429865473?s=20&t=iw-MdsDUIYhcmY5I02vuaA. Accessed 16 Jan. 2023.

7. Twitter, https://twitter.com/elonmusk/status/15768463 97793787904?s=20&t=iw-MdsDUIYhcmY5I02vuaA. Accessed 16 Jan. 2023.

8. Kestenbaum, David. "Making a Mark with Rockets and Roadsters." www.Npr.Org, https://www.npr. org/2007/08/09/12484430/making-a-mark-with-rockets-and-roadsters. Accessed 16 Jan. 2023.

9. New China. Jack Ma and Elon Musk Hold Debate in Shanghai. YouTube, 29 Aug. 2019, https://www. youtube.com/watch?v=f3lUEnMaiAU.

10. "The Great Filter: A Possible Solution to the Fermi Paradox | Astronomy.com." Astronomy.com, 20 Nov. 2020, https://astronomy.com/news/2020/11/the-great-filter-a-possible-solution-to-the-fermi-paradox.

11. "SpaceX." SpaceX, http://www.spacex.com. Accessed 21 Apr. 2023.

12. Lung, Doug. "SpaceX to Attempt Landing Falcon 9 First Stage on Ocean Platform | TV Tech." TV Tech, 19 Dec. 2014, https://www.tvtechnology.com/opinions/spacex-to-attempt-landing-falcon-9-first-stage-on-ocean-platform.
13. Thompson, Amy. "SpaceX's Elon Musk and His Plans to Send 1 Million People to Mars." TESLARATI, 26 Jan. 2020, https://www.teslarati.com/spacex-ceo-elon-musk-plan-colonize-mars-1-million-people/.
14. Twitter, https://twitter.com/elonmusk/status/1400008467822399490. Accessed 18 Jan. 2023.

THE NATURE OF THE MEDIA

1. "Watch Tucker Carlson Today: Season 3, Episode 39, 'Elon Musk' Online - Fox Nation." Fox Nation, https://nation.foxnews.com/watch/368a7207ca9bea989e-05c23d74583ef5. Accessed 21 Apr. 2023.
2. Twitter, https://twitter.com/elonmusk/status/15523248 11153707018?s=20&t=iw-MdsDUIYhcmY5I02vuaA. Accessed 16 Jan. 2023.
3. Twitter, https://twitter.com/elonmusk/status/15323615 9361847298?s=20&t=iw-MdsDUIYhcmY5I02vuaA. Accessed 16 Jan. 2023.
4. Twitter, https://twitter.com/elonmusk/status/14908329 93258450944?s=20&t=iw-MdsDUIYhcmY5I02vuaA. Accessed 16 Jan. 2023.
5. Twitter, https://twitter.com/elonmusk/status/12791487 45016344577?s=20&t=iw-MdsDUIYhcmY5I02vuaA. Accessed 16 Jan. 2023.

6. Twitter, https://twitter.com/elonmusk/status/14999829
   13949081600?s=20&t=iw-MdsDUIYhcmY5I02vuaA.
   Accessed 16 Jan. 2023.
7. Twitter, https://twitter.com/elonmusk/status/15911383
   16862488578?s=20&t=iw-MdsDUIYhcmY5I02vuaA.
   Accessed 16 Jan. 2023.
8. Gulik, Greg. Elon Musk Interviewed by Fareed Zakaria
   CNN. YouTube, 26 Nov. 2013, https://www.youtube.
   com/watch?v=zet-X_7MG_Q.
9. Twitter, https://twitter.com/elonmusk/sta-
   tus/1586852118539145216?s=20&t=JDx22txj_
   QiFtQmTiP-KeA. Accessed 16 Jan. 2023.
10. Twitter, https://twitter.com/elonmusk/sta-
    tus/1591121142961799168?s=20&t=JDx22txj_
    QiFtQmTiP-KeA. Accessed 16 Jan. 2023.
11. Twitter, https://twitter.com/elonmusk/status/15303391
    99232135168?s=20&t=iw-MdsDUIYhcmY5I02vuaA.
    Accessed 16 Jan. 2023.
12. "Musk Talks Early Troubles, Tesla's Future Video from
    Automotive News." Automotive News, 16 Jan. 2015,
    https://www.autonews.com/article/20150116/VID-
    EO/150119764/musk-talks-early-troubles-tesla-s-fu-
    ture.
13. Twitter, https://twitter.com/elonmusk/sta-
    tus/1582987988233256961?s=20&t=JDx22txj_
    QiFtQmTiP-KeA. Accessed 16 Jan. 2023.
14. Twitter, https://twitter.com/elonmusk/status/14908318
    91640946689?s=20&t=iw-MdsDUIYhcmY5I02vuaA.
    Accessed 16 Jan. 2023.
15. Twitter, https://twitter.com/elonmusk/status/12854439
    97654122496?s=20&t=iw-MdsDUIYhcmY5I02vuaA.
    Accessed 16 Jan. 2023.

16. Elon Musk: A Future Worth Getting Excited about | TED | Tesla Texas Gigafactory Interview. YouTube, 18 Apr. 2022, https://www.youtube.com/watch?v=YRvf-00NooN8.

17. Twitter, https://twitter.com/elonmusk/status/1522593007211466753?s=20&t=iw-MdsDUIYhcmY5I02vuaA. Accessed 16 Jan. 2023.

18. Pranksters Pretending to Be Laid-off Twitter Employees Leave San Francisco HQ | AFP. YouTube, https://www.youtube.com/watch?v=XKyKKWxr5mQ. Accessed 21 Apr. 2023.

19. Elon Musk Talks Twitter, Tesla and How His Brain Works — Live at TED2022. YouTube, https://www.youtube.com/watch?v=cdZZpaB2kDM. Accessed 21 Apr. 2023.

20. Twitter, https://twitter.com/elonmusk/status/1591876240830504960?s=20&t=JDx22txj_QiFtQmTiP-KeA. Accessed 16 Jan. 2023.

21. Twitter, https://twitter.com/elonmusk/status/1553988167912620033?s=20&t=JDx22txj_QiFtQmTiP-KeA. Accessed 16 Jan. 2023.

THE NATURE OF POLITICS

1. Twitter, https://twitter.com/elonmusk/status/1529864162804899843?s=20&t=KF7VeRnELYAzvM573Z9I6g. Accessed 16 Jan. 2023.

2. Twitter, https://twitter.com/elonmusk/status/1589997215862652929?s=20&t=dWAQxXM2kSrTuSxmnJ5JaA. Accessed 16 Jan. 2023.

3. Twitter, https://twitter.com/elonmusk/status/1605219914813673473?s=20&t=3L8JH3Ko-Lp-7CQKS3fql5A. Accessed 10 Feb. 2023.
4. Twitter, https://twitter.com/elonmusk/status/1487861890730496001?s=20. Accessed 21 Apr. 2023.
5. Université Paris 1 Panthéon-Sorbonne. Conversation Avec Elon Musk à Paris 1 Panthéon-Sorbonne. YouTube, 3 Dec. 2015, https://www.youtube.com/watch?v=BMskI6G9ty0.
6. Twitter, https://twitter.com/elonmusk/status/1594750738940383232?s=20&t=GOryLV-3Qsm-BuN_eTv8fMQ. Accessed 16 Jan. 2023.
7. Lambert, Fred. "Tesla Slips, but Still Owns Two-Thirds of the US EV Market." Electrek, 11 Oct. 2022, https://electrek.co/2022/10/11/tesla-slips-owns-two-thirds-us-ev-market/.
8. Yahoo! Finance. White House Press Secretary Jen Psaki Holds Press Briefing. YouTube, 5 Aug. 2021, https://www.youtube.com/watch?v=SeCF77Bwgaw.
9. Twitter, https://twitter.com/elonmusk/status/1529977466940542977?s=20&t=KF7VeRnELYAz-vM573Z9I6g. Accessed 16 Jan. 2023.

YOU ARE WRONG

1. Twitter, https://twitter.com/elonmusk/status/1569381543184941060?s=20&t=sOBGkjFaenGyYn-G6W1v0FQ. Accessed 22 Apr. 2023.
2. Mohammad Al Gergawi in a Conversation with Elon Musk during WGS17. YouTube, https://www.youtube.com/watch?v=rCoFKUJ_8Yo. Accessed 22 Apr. 2023.

3. Elon Musk Advice - Critical Thinking (Success Rule). YouTube, https://www.youtube.com/shorts/Ndiv1k5uSMg. Accessed 22 Apr. 2023.
4. Clean Tech Summit 2011 - IPO Spotlight with Elon Musk. YouTube, https://www.youtube.com/watch?v=hTBZGWEzR_E. Accessed 22 Apr. 2023.
5. Joe Rogan Experience #1169 - Elon Musk. YouTube, https://www.youtube.com/watch?v=ycPr5-27vSI. Accessed 22 Apr. 2023.
6. Elon Musk Answers Your Questions! | SXSW 2018. YouTube, https://www.youtube.com/watch?v=kzlUyrc-cbos. Accessed 22 Apr. 2023.

GIVE YOUR FOLLOWERS A NORTH STAR

1. Harris, Paul. "Elon Musk: 'I'm Planning to Retire to Mars.'" The Observer, 31 July 2010. The Guardian, https://www.theguardian.com/technology/2010/aug/01/elon-musk-spacex-rocket-mars.
2. The Mars Society. Elon Musk - 2020 Mars Society Virtual Convention. YouTube, 16 Oct. 2020, https://www.youtube.com/watch?v=y5Aw6WG4Dww.
3. "The Mission of Tesla | Tesla." Tesla, https://www.tesla.com/blog/mission-tesla. Accessed 16 Jan. 2023.
4. Megan Gannon. "SpaceX's Elon Musk and Joseph Gordon-Levitt Talk Manned Mars Missions (Video)." Yahoo News, 1 Feb. 2014, https://news.yahoo.com/spacex-39-elon-musk-joseph-gordon-levitt-talk-124915255.html.
5. Twitter, https://twitter.com/elonmusk/status/1194823241673723904?s=20&t=iw-MdsDUIYhcmY5I02vuaA. Accessed 16 Jan. 2023.

6. Twitter, https://twitter.com/elonmusk/status/13741578
05406523397?s=20&t=iw-MdsDUIYhcmY5I02vuaA.
Accessed 16 Jan. 2023.

7. Twitter, https://twitter.com/elonmusk/status/15169773
23576381441?s=20&t=iw-MdsDUIYhcmY5I02vuaA.
Accessed 22 Apr. 2023.

8. Elon Alerts. Elon Musk Interviewed about Twitter by
Robin Wheeler—9 November 2022. YouTube, 9 Nov.
2022, https://www.youtube.com/watch?v=Gqh-
FQpRZ_5U.

9. Khan Academy. Elon Musk - CEO of Tesla Motors and
SpaceX | Entrepreneurship | Khan Academy. YouTube,
22 Apr. 2013, https://www.youtube.com/watch?v=-
vDwzmJpI4io.

10. PowerfulJRE. Joe Rogan Experience #1425 - Garrett
Reisman. YouTube, 7 Feb. 2020, https://www.youtube.
com/watch?v=3RG5pXTpLBI

11. Dyches, Preston. "What Is the North Star and How Do
You Find It?" NASA Solar System Exploration, 28 July
2021, https://solarsystem.nasa.gov/news/1944/what-is-
the-north-star-and-how-do-you-find-it/.

THE NECESSITY OF HUMOR

1. "Elon Musk How To Make A Small Fortune In The
Rocket Business! #shorts #money #finance #business."
YouTube, 30 Nov. 2022, https://www.youtube.com/
shorts/EXXEqmyrbbY.

2. Elon Musk | SXSW Live 2013 | SXSW ON. YouTube,
10 Mar. 2015, https://www.youtube.com/watch?v=Le-
QMWdOMa-A.

3. Elon Musk Out of Context. Do You Ever Think about Electric Cars? YouTube, 15 Apr. 2021, https://www. youtube.com/watch?v=Z0r-nD-Ksmo.

4. Twitter, https://twitter.com/elonmusk/status/14617513 44415617025?s=20&t=iw-MdsDUIYhcmY5I02vuaA. Accessed 16 Jan. 2023.

5. Twitter, https://twitter.com/elonmusk/status/576140759281238017?s=20&t=uUtJCtT4P5eU-PZPr5X7tdA. Accessed 16 Jan. 2023.

6. Heath, Chris. "How Elon Musk Plans on Reinventing the World (and Mars) | GQ." GQ, GQ, 11 Dec. 2015, https://www.gq.com/story/elon-musk-mars-spacex-tesla-interview.

7. Springer, Axel. Axel Springer Award 2020. YouTube, 1 Dec. 2020, https://www.youtube.com/watch?v=AF-2HXId2Xhg.

8. Twitter, https://twitter.com/elonmusk/status/1588427451255836672?s=20&t=iw-MdsDUIYhcmY5I02vuaA. Accessed 16 Jan. 2023.

9. Twitter, https://twitter.com/elonmusk/status/1588750686006947840?s=20&t=JDx22txj_QiFtQmTiP-KeA. Accessed 16 Jan. 2023.

10. Elon Musk Facts. Elon Musk: Aliens Land with PARA-CHUTES. YouTube, 9 June 2022, https://www. youtube.com/watch?v=uXFDHsJeJgU.

11. Twitter, https://twitter.com/elonmusk/status/1599812881708896259. Accessed 18 Jan. 2023.

12. Twitter, https://twitter.com/elonmusk/status/1599812881708896259?s=20. Accessed 22 Apr. 2023.

13. Twitter, https://twitter.com/elonmusk/status/1587290042162204673?s=20&t=JDx22txj_QiFtQmTiP-KeA. Accessed 16 Jan. 2023.

14. Twitter, https://twitter.com/elonmusk/status/1583503854322130945?s=20&t=JDx22txj_QiFtQmTiP-KeA. Accessed 16 Jan. 2023.

15. Stories, Startup. Elon Musk "Ford Is Killing SEX." YouTube, 15 Dec. 2021, https://www.youtube.com/watch?v=RKlvqpAFSnk.

16. Twitter, https://twitter.com/elonmusk/status/1580304724082843648?s=20&t=JDx22txj_QiFtQmTiP-KeA. Accessed 16 Jan. 2023.

17. Twitter, https://twitter.com/elonmusk/status/1537219088283381760?s=20&t=JDx22txj_QiFtQmTiP-KeA. Accessed 16 Jan. 2023.

18. Twitter, https://twitter.com/elonmusk/status/1535749847944511490?s=20&t=JDx22txj_QiFtQmTiP-KeA. Accessed 16 Jan. 2023.

19. Twitter, https://twitter.com/elonmusk/status/1519480761749016577?s=20&t=iw-MdsDUIYhcmY5I02vuaA. Accessed 16 Jan. 2023.

20. Elon Musk Reveals His Knowledge on Aliens, Challenges Putin to UFC, and Predicts WW3. YouTube, 5 Aug. 2022, https://www.youtube.com/watch?v=fXS_gkWAIs0.

21. Joe Rogan Clips - Elon Musk Explains His Flamethrower Idea. YouTube, 7 Sept. 2018, https://www.youtube.com/watch?v=HfqtKPP2_6M.

WORK

1. Elon Musk Zone. "DON'T MAKE THIS MISTAKE!"
   — Elon Musk. YouTube, 26 May 2021, https://www.
   youtube.com/watch?v=jhVllI0tde8.
2. Daum, Meghan. "Elon Musk, CEO of Tesla and
   SpaceX, Wants to Change How (and Where) Humans
   Live | Vogue." Vogue, Vogue, 21 Sept. 2015, https://
   www.vogue.com/article/elon-musk-profile-entrepre-
   neur-spacex-tesla-motors.
3. Boes, Corrin. CHM Revolutionaries: An Evening with
   Elon Musk. YouTube, 24 Jan. 2018, https://www.
   youtube.com/watch?v=dQIQqOZqGIA.
4. Chispa Motivation. AGAINST ALL ODDS - Elon
   Musk (Motivational Video). YouTube, 18 June 2019,
   https://www.youtube.com/watch?v=k9zTr2MAFRg.
5. Carmichael, Evan. SUCCESS Has Nothing to DO
   With LUCK! | Elon Musk MOTIVATION. YouTube,
   25 Dec. 2020, https://www.youtube.com/
   watch?v=1AU819P7Bk4.
6. Prime. Elon Musk Gives Jay Leno A Tour of SpaceX |
   Watch The Full Ep Wed 10p ET. YouTube, 16 Sept.
   2022, https://www.youtube.com/watch?v=wluBlr1j4qk.
7. Beach Bali Channel. Elon Musk with Nadiem Makarim
   Full Live Interview at Kampus Merdeka Festival | G20
   Indonesia 2022. YouTube, 14 Nov. 2022, https://www.
   youtube.com/watch?v=Xp-fZcMOsdw.

DO COOL THINGS

1. Twitter, https://twitter.com/erdayastronaut/sta-
   tus/1218939014146863104. Accessed 16 Jan. 2023.

2. McHatton. Elon Musk : Living Legend of Aviation. YouTube, 19 Jan. 2010, https://www.youtube.com/watch?v=lvWyoKqB78o.

3. Twitter, https://twitter.com/elonmusk/status/1575508498430820352?s=20&t=JDx22txj_QiFtQmTiP-KeA. Accessed 16 Jan. 2023.

4. Twitter, https://twitter.com/elonmusk/status/1582997766741327873?s=20&t=JDx22txj_QiFtQmTiP-KeA. Accessed 16 Jan. 2023.

5. Springer, Axel. Axel Springer Award 2020. YouTube, 1 Dec. 2020, https://www.youtube.com/watch?v=AF-2HXId2Xhg.

6. zeitgeist08. Elon Musk, CEO and CTO, Space Exploration Technologies Corp (SpaceX), Peter Diamandis, CEO, X Prize Foundation and John Doerr, Venture Capital, Kleiner Perkins Caufield & Byers. YouTube, 22 Sept. 2008, https://www.youtube.com/watch?v=s3Rl-CVtQ6mA.

7. Elon Musk Viral Videos. Elon Musk's Legendary Commencement Speech. YouTube, 5 June 2018, https://www.youtube.com/watch?v=MxZpaJK74Y4.

8. Every Elon Musk Video. Tesla Q2 2016 Earnings Call | Bullish despite Bad Results (2016.8.3) AUDIO. YouTube, 7 Mar. 2022, https://www.youtube.com/watch?v=VeZlHJKbH0c.

9. PowerfulJRE. Joe Rogan Experience #1169 - Elon Musk. YouTube, 7 Sept. 2018, https://www.youtube.com/watch?v=ycPr5-27vSI.

10. Ciaccia, Chris. "NASA Has Certified Elon Musk's SpaceX to Carry Astronauts, Ending Its Reliance on Russia" Fox News, 11 Nov. 2020, https://www.foxnews.com/science/nasa-elon-musk-spacex-carry-astronauts-russia.

11. Travis, Matthew. Postlanding Telecon With Elon Musk - Falcon 9 v1.1 RTF Orbcomm OG2 M2. YouTube, 23 Dec. 2015, https://www.youtube.com/watch?v=L-gNekVW0pps.

12. Travis, Matthew. Postlanding Telecon With Elon Musk - Falcon 9 v1.1 RTF Orbcomm OG2 M2. YouTube, 23 Dec. 2015, https://www.youtube.com/watch?v=L-gNekVW0pps.

13. Elon Musk Videos. Elon Musk Is Over the Moon after Falcon 1 Reaches Orbit 2008. YouTube, 5 Nov. 2015, https://www.youtube.com/watch?v=fuK8RLik1zU.

14. PowerfulJRE. Joe Rogan Experience #1470 - Elon Musk. YouTube, 7 May 2020, https://www.youtube.com/watch?v=RcYjXbSJBN8.

15. Tesla Xfinity-Sustainable Progress. Tesla Model X Launch | Full Unveiling Event by Elon Musk. YouTube, 1 Oct. 2015, https://www.youtube.com/watch?v=eWIt-4Ze7r9Y.

16. National Lab. ISSDC 2015 - A Conversation with Elon Musk. YouTube, 8 July 2015, https://www.youtube.com/watch?v=ZmEg95wPiVU.

17. shazmosushi. Elon Musk's 2003 Stanford University Entrepreneurial Thought Leaders Lecture. YouTube, 12 July 2013, https://www.youtube.com/watch?v=afZ-TrfvB2AQ.

18. Tesla. Tesla Unveils Model 3. YouTube, 1 Apr. 2016, https://www.youtube.com/watch?v=Q4VGQPk2Dl8.

19. Tesla. Tesla Unveils Model 3. YouTube, 1 Apr. 2016, https://www.youtube.com/watch?v=Q4VGQPk2Dl8.
20. Elliott, Hannah. "At Home With Elon Musk: The (Soon-to-Be) Bachelor Billionaire." Forbes, Forbes, 26 Mar. 2012, https://www.forbes.com/sites/hannahelliott/2012/03/26/at-home-with-elon-musk-the-soon-to-be-bachelor-billionaire/?sh=54149070729b.
21. Mornings. Why Tesla CEO Elon Musk Doesn't Consider Himself a Businessman. YouTube, 13 Apr. 2018, https://www.youtube.com/watch?v=jQMHEXquK9A.
22. Khan Academy. Elon Musk - CEO of Tesla Motors and SpaceX | Entrepreneurship | Khan Academy. YouTube, 22 Apr. 2013, https://www.youtube.com/watch?v=-vDwzmJpI4io.
23. Twitter, https://twitter.com/elonmusk/status/1598754422942728194?s=20&t=JDx22txj_QiFtQmTiP-KeA. Accessed 16 Jan. 2023.
24. Prime. ELON MUSK, JAY LENO AND THE 2021 CYBERTRUCK (FULL SEGMENT) | Jay Leno's Garage. YouTube, 28 May 2020, https://www.youtube.com/watch?v=25ZuKkbHdqM.
25. Elon Musk Reveals His Knowledge on Aliens, Challenges Putin to UFC, and Predicts WW3. YouTube, 5 Aug. 2022, https://www.youtube.com/watch?v=fXS_gkWAIs0.

ON UTILITY

1. Swisher, Kara. "Elon Musk: 'A.I. Doesn't Need to Hate Us to Destroy Us.'" www.nytimes.com, Sway, 28 Sept. 2020, https://www.nytimes.com/2020/09/28/opinion/sway-kara-swisher-elon-musk.html.

2. Outcast Motivation. MIND BLOWING WORK ETHIC - Elon Musk Motivational Video. YouTube, 14 Nov. 2021, https://www.youtube.com/watch?v=-U5d-EdWouDY.

3. The Space Archive. RAW Elon Musk Interview from Air Warfare Symposium 2020. YouTube, 2 Mar. 2020, https://www.youtube.com/watch?v=sp8smJFaKYE.

4. Space Policy Politics. Elon Musk, Satellite 2020 Conference, Washington DC, March 9, 2020. YouTube, 24 Mar. 2020, https://www.youtube.com/watch?v=ywPqL-Cc9zBU.

5. Elon Musk Videos. Elon Musk and Bill Gates Discuss A.I., Entrepreneurship and More 2015. YouTube, 25 Nov. 2015, https://www.youtube.com/watch?v=OLi0seDZoaI.

6. Twitter, https://twitter.com/elonmusk/status/15043499 78487324672?s=20&t=iw-MdsDUIYhcmY5I02vuaA. Accessed 16 Jan. 2023.

7. DROdio. Elon Musk Interview by Sarah Lacy + TheFunded FounderShowcase (Part 3 of 3). YouTube, 6 Aug. 2010, https://www.youtube.com/watch?v=1N-eqRhgtC1o.

8. Davis, Johnny. "One More Giant Leap." The Telegraph, 4AD, https://www.telegraph.co.uk/culture/3666994/One-more-giant-leap.html

9. Elon Musk : How to Build the Future. YouTube, https://www.youtube.com/watch?v=tnBQmEqBCY0. Accessed 10 Feb. 2023.

10. Stanford eCorner. Elon Musk: Elon Musk's Vision for the Future [Entire Talk]. YouTube, 11 Dec. 2015, https://www.youtube.com/watch?v=SVk1hb0ZOrE.

11. Heath, Chris. "How Elon Musk Plans on Reinventing the World (and Mars) | GQ." GQ, GQ, 11 Dec. 2015, https://www.gq.com/story/elon-musk-mars-spacex-tesla-interview.

12. Twitter, https://twitter.com/elonmusk/status/1563944510358712321?s=20&t=iw-MdsDUIYhcmY5I02vuaA. Accessed 16 Jan. 2023.

13. Twitter, https://twitter.com/elonmusk/status/1584906280082219009?s=20&t=iw-MdsDUIYhcmY5I02vuaA. Accessed 16 Jan. 2023.

14. Twitter, https://twitter.com/elonmusk/status/1508624262826930179. Accessed 17 Jan. 2023.

15. Twitter, https://twitter.com/elonmusk/status/1546518224887496705?s=20&t=JDx22txj_QiFtQmTiP-KeA. Accessed 16 Jan. 2023.

BUREAUCRACY IS BAD

1. Tesla Founder and CEO Elon Musk Shares Energy Vision at 2015 EEI Annual Convention. YouTube, 11 June 2015, https://www.youtube.com/watch?v=UKT2tKmVk6g.

2. Twitter, https://twitter.com/amogh42/status/1592916218968956928/photo/1. Accessed 16 Jan. 2023.

3. Twitter, https://twitter.com/amogh42/status/1592916218968956928/photo/11. Accessed 16 Jan. 2023.

4. Twitter, https://twitter.com/amogh42/status/1592916218968956928/photo/11. Accessed 16 Jan. 2023.

5. Twitter, https://twitter.com/amogh42/status/1592916218968956928/photo/11. Accessed 16 Jan. 2023.
6. Twitter, https://twitter.com/amogh42/status/1592916218968956928/photo/11. Accessed 16 Jan. 2023.
7. Twitter, https://twitter.com/amogh42/status/1592916218968956928/photo/11. Accessed 16 Jan. 2023.
8. Twitter, https://twitter.com/amogh42/status/1592916218968956928/photo/11. Accessed 16 Jan. 2023.
9. The caroverse. Space X Tour | Space X Factory Tour By Elon Musk. YouTube, 25 June 2020, https://www.youtube.com/watch?v=ibsgicbKCK4.
10. Twitter, https://twitter.com/elonmusk/status/1532403096680288256?s=20&t=GOryLV-3Qsm-BuN_eTv8fMQ. Accessed 16 Jan. 2023.
11. Anderson, Chris. "Elon Musk's Mission to Mars | WIRED." WIRED, WIRED, 21 Oct. 2012, https://www.wired.com/2012/10/ff-elon-musk-qa/.
12. Wall Street Journal. Elon Musk on Tesla, SpaceX and Why He Left Silicon Valley | WSJ. YouTube, 9 Dec. 2020, https://www.youtube.com/watch?v=V1nQFot-zQMQ.
13. Twitter, https://twitter.com/elonmusk/status/1313850036564963328?s=20&t=i9p1CfAOCFxd-KEOhf-Iddg. Accessed 16 Jan. 2023.
14. Twitter, https://twitter.com/elonmusk/status/1450857138906087433?s=20&t=iw-MdsDUIYhcmY5I02vuaA. Accessed 16 Jan. 2023.

15. Boes, Corrin. CHM Revolutionaries: An Evening with Elon Musk. YouTube, 24 Jan. 2018, https://www.youtube.com/watch?v=dQIQqOZqGIA.

16. Elon Musk on Tesla, SpaceX and Why He Left Silicon Valley | WSJ. YouTube, https://www.youtube.com/watch?v=V1nQFotzQMQ. Accessed 18 Jan. 2023.

17. Boes, Corrin. CHM Revolutionaries: An Evening with Elon Musk. YouTube, 24 Jan. 2018, https://www.youtube.com/watch?v=dQIQqOZqGIA.

18. Twitter, https://twitter.com/elonmusk/status/14617847 20652525576?s=20&t=iw-MdsDUIYhcmY5I02vuaA. Accessed 16 Jan. 2023.

19. Anderson, Chris. "Elon Musk's Mission to Mars | WIRED." WIRED, WIRED, 21 Oct. 2012, https://www.wired.com/2012/10/ff-elon-musk-qa/.

20. Elon Musk Answers Your Questions! | SXSW 2018. YouTube, 12 Mar. 2018, https://www.youtube.com/watch?v=kzlUyrccbos.

21. The Space Archive. RAW Elon Musk Interview from Air Warfare Symposium 2020. YouTube, 2 Mar. 2020, https://www.youtube.com/watch?v=sp8smJFaKYE.

22. Everyday Astronaut. Talking to Elon Musk and Jim Bridenstine about SpaceX Fly Astronauts for the 1st Time! #DM2. YouTube, 27 May 2020, https://www.youtube.com/watch?v=p4ZLysa9Qqg.

SCALING TECHNOLOGY

1. Brownlee, Marques. Talking Tech with Elon Musk! YouTube, 18 Aug. 2018, https://www.youtube.com/watch?v=MevKTPN4ozw.

2. "The Mission of Tesla | Tesla." Tesla, https://www.tesla.com/blog/mission-tesla. Accessed 16 Jan. 2023.

3. Elon Musk at Tesla Shareholders Meeting 2016 -Part 2-. YouTube, https://www.youtube.com/watch?v=Ezu54pn5I4w. Accessed 18 Jan. 2023.

4. Swisher, Kara. "Elon Musk: 'A.I. Doesn't Need to Hate Us to Destroy Us.'" www.nytimes.com, Sway, 28 Sept. 2020, https://www.nytimes.com/2020/09/28/opinion/sway-kara-swisher-elon-musk.html.

5. Twitter, https://twitter.com/elonmusk/status/1308284091142266881?s=20&t=KF7VeRnELYAzvM573Z9I6g. Accessed 16 Jan. 2023.

6. Elon Musk at Tesla Shareholders Meeting 2016 -Part 2. YouTube, https://www.youtube.com/watch?v=Ezu54pn5I4w. Accessed 22 Apr. 2023.

7. Twitter, https://twitter.com/elonmusk/status/1389102532706848768?s=20&t=KF7VeRnELYAzvM573Z9I6g. Accessed 16 Jan. 2023.

8. Reingold, Jennifer. "Hondas in Space." Fast Company, 5 Feb. 2005, www.fastcompany.com.

9. Computer History Museum. CHM Revolutionaries: An Evening with Elon Musk. YouTube, 5 Feb. 2013, https://www.youtube.com/watch?v=AHHwXUm3iIg.

10. The Space Archive. RAW Elon Musk Interview from Air Warfare Symposium 2020. YouTube, 2 Mar. 2020, https://www.youtube.com/watch?v=sp8smJFaKYE.

11. Twitter, https://twitter.com/elonmusk/status/1473683749518950424?s=20&t=KF7VeRnELYAzvM573Z9I6g. Accessed 16 Jan. 2023.

12. Outcast Motivation. MIND BLOWING WORK ETHIC - Elon Musk Motivational Video. YouTube, 14 Nov. 2021, https://www.youtube.com/watch?v=-U5d-EdWouDY.

13. Musk, Elon. "Master Plan, Part Deux | Tesla." Tesla, https://www.tesla.com/blog/master-plan-part-deux. Accessed 16 Jan. 2023.

MERITOCRACY RULES

1. Twitter, https://twitter.com/elonmusk/status/1522609829553971200?s=20&t=KF7VeRnELYAz-vM573Z9I6g. Accessed 16 Jan. 2023.

2. Munro Live. Elon Musk Interview: 1-on-1 with Sandy Munro. YouTube, 2 Feb. 2021, https://www.youtube.com/watch?v=YAtLTLiqNwg.

3. Channel 007. Elon Musk - MIT Aeronautics and Astronautics Department Interview. YouTube, 9 Aug. 2020, https://www.youtube.com/watch?v=qlClk-9G15i4.

4. Heath, Alex. "Everything Elon Musk Told Twitter Employees in His First Company Meeting - The Verge." The Verge, The Verge, 11 Nov. 2022, https://www.theverge.com/2022/11/10/23452196/elon-musk-twitter-employee-meeting-q-and-a.

5. Twitter, https://twitter.com/elonmusk/status/1591580235132465153?s=20. Accessed 22 Apr. 2023.

6. Twitter, https://twitter.com/elonmusk/status/1532715028742385668?s=20&t=KF7VeRnELYAz-vM573Z9I6g. Accessed 16 Jan. 2023.

7. PowerfulJRE. Joe Rogan Experience #1169 - Elon Musk. YouTube, 7 Sept. 2018, https://www.youtube.com/watch?v=ycPr5-27vSI.

8. Hoffman, Carl. "Elon Musk, the Rocket Man With a Sweet Ride | Science| Smithsonian Magazine." Smithsonian Magazine, Smithsonian Magazine, 1 Dec. 2012, https://www.smithsonianmag.com/science-nature/elon-musk-the-rocket-man-with-a-sweet-ride-136059680/.

9. Inc. A Conversation with Tesla CEO Elon Musk | Inc. Magazine. YouTube, 13 Nov. 2015, https://www.youtube.com/watch?v=Xcut1JfTMoM.

10. Elon Musk Talks Twitter, Tesla and How His Brain Works — Live at TED2022. YouTube, 14 Apr. 2022, https://www.youtube.com/watch?v=cdZZpaB2kDM.

11. Twitter, https://twitter.com/elonmusk/status/1587867451806695431?s=20&t=JDx22txj_QiFtQmTiP-KeA. Accessed 16 Jan. 2023.

12. Twitter, https://twitter.com/elonmusk/status/1594748242939494431?s=20&t=JDx22txj_QiFtQmTiP-KeA. Accessed 16 Jan. 2023.

13. O'Reilly. Conversation with Elon Musk (Tesla Motors) - Web 2.0 Summit 08. YouTube, 11 Nov. 2008, https://www.youtube.com/watch?v=gVwmNaPsxLc.

RATE OF FIXING MISTAKES

1. Elon Musk Videos. Elon Musk Talks about a New Type of School He Created for His Kids 2015. YouTube, 30 Nov. 2015, https://www.youtube.com/watch?v=y-6909DjNLCM.

2. Elon Musk Videos. Elon Musk Talks about a New Type of School He Created for His Kids 2015. YouTube, 30 Nov. 2015, https://www.youtube.com/watch?v=y-6909DjNLCM.

3. Elon Musk Videos. Elon Musk Talks Autopilot & Model X - Q3 2015 Earnings Call 2015 (AUDIO). YouTube, 10 Dec. 2015, https://www.youtube.com/watch?v=u-uCZHK5Oik

4. Elon Alerts. Elon Musk Interviewed about Twitter by Robin Wheeler—9 November 2022. YouTube, 9 Nov. 2022, https://www.youtube.com/watch?v=Gqh-FQpRZ_5U.

DOING THE RIGHT THING

1. Swisher, Kara. "Elon Musk: 'A.I. Doesn't Need to Hate Us to Destroy Us.'" www.nytimes.com, Sway, 28 Sept. 2020, https://www.nytimes.com/2020/09/28/opinion/sway-kara-swisher-elon-musk.html.

2. Financial Times. Elon Musk Talks to the FT about Twitter, Tesla and Trump | FT. YouTube, 11 May 2022, https://www.youtube.com/watch?v=2cNLh1gfQIk.

3. Michael. 2016 Tesla Annual Shareholder Meeting. YouTube, 17 Jan. 2020, https://www.youtube.com/watch?v=NOAu_G3f0eA.

4. Elon and Kimbal Musk Interview. YouTube, 7 Jan. 2014, https://www.youtube.com/watch?v=1u6kQIzza-PI.

5. Elon Musk Talks Twitter, Tesla and How His Brain Works — Live at TED2022. YouTube, 14 Apr. 2022, https://www.youtube.com/watch?v=cdZZpaB2kDM.

6. Elon Musk Has Open Sourced the Patents on Tesla Electric Cars. YouTube, 10 Dec. 2018, https://www.youtube.com/watch?v=WyTzRnGSlcI.

7. "All Our Patent Are Belong To You | Tesla." Tesla, https://www.tesla.com/blog/all-our-patent-are-belong-you. Accessed 16 Jan. 2023.

8. The Space Archive. RAW Elon Musk Interview from Air Warfare Symposium 2020. YouTube, 2 Mar. 2020, https://www.youtube.com/watch?v=sp8smJFaKYE.

9. "Master Plan, Part Deux | Tesla." Tesla, https://www.tesla.com/blog/master-plan-part-deux. Accessed 16 Jan. 2023.

10. Elon Musk 2015 Detriot Auto Show Full Interview. YouTube, https://www.youtube.com/watch?v=LTbQF-dyizGQ. Accessed 22 Apr. 2023.

11. Transcripts. "Tesla Motors (TSLA) Elon Reeve Musk on Q1 2016 Results - Earnings Call Transcript | Seeking Alpha." SeekingAlpha, Seeking Alpha, 5 May 2016, https://seekingalpha.com/article/3971543-tesla-motors-tsla-elon-reeve-musk-on-q1-2016-results-earnings-call-transcript.

12. MacKenzie, Angus. "Elon Musk Unplugged: Tesla CEO's Future of the Car Keynote Highlights" Motor-Trend, 13 May 2022, https://www.motortrend.com/news/elon-musk-financial-times-keynote-interview/#:~:text=We've%20already%20opened%20Tesla,option%20to%20Superchargers%20in%20U.

13. "To the People of New Jersey | Tesla." Tesla, https://www.tesla.com/blog/people-new-jersey. Accessed 16 Jan. 2023.

14. Musk, Elon. Elon Musk Interview with Billionaire Investment Legend Ron Baron. YouTube, 19 Sept. 2016, https://www.youtube.com/watch?v=1K6PDvdP-Dkg.

15. "Response to Mercury News Article, Entitled 'The Hidden Workforce Expanding Tesla's Factory.'" Tesla, https://www.tesla.com/blog/response-mercury-news-article-hidden-workforce-expanding-teslas-factory. Accessed 16 Jan. 2023.

16. "2016 Shareholder Meeting." Tesla, https://www.tesla.com/2016shareholdermeeting. Accessed 22 Apr. 2023.

17. Twitter, https://twitter.com/elonmusk/status/1595563761402015744?s=20&t=JDx22txj_QiFtQmTiP-KeA. Accessed 16 Jan. 2023.

18. Twitter, https://twitter.com/elonmusk/status/1596275526259425280?s=20&t=JDx22txj_QiFtQmTiP-KeA. Accessed 16 Jan. 2023.

19. Twitter, https://twitter.com/elonmusk/status/1595671290421170179?s=20&t=JDx22txj_QiFtQmTiP-KeA. Accessed 16 Jan. 2023.

20. Twitter, https://twitter.com/elonmusk/status/1595534031545765890?s=20&t=JDx22txj_QiFtQmTiP-KeA. Accessed 16 Jan. 2023.

21. Twitter, https://twitter.com/elonmusk/status/1588666492572553216?s=20&t=JDx22txj_QiFtQmTiP-KeA. Accessed 16 Jan. 2023.

22. Twitter, https://twitter.com/elonmusk/status/1586105918143406080?s=20&t=JDx22txj_QiFtQmTiP-KeA. Accessed 16 Jan. 2023.

23. Twitter, https://twitter.com/elonmusk/status/1584715136547573762?s=20&t=JDx22txj_QiFtQmTiP-KeA. Accessed 16 Jan. 2023.

24. Elon Alerts. Elon Musk Interviewed about Twitter by Robin Wheeler—9 November 2022. YouTube, 9 Nov. 2022, https://www.youtube.com/watch?v=Gqh-FQpRZ_5U.

25. Twitter, https://twitter.com/elonmusk/status/1587498907336118274?s=20&t=KF7VeRnELYAz-vM573Z9I6g. Accessed 16 Jan. 2023.

26. Elon Musk | SXSW Live 2013 | SXSW ON. YouTube, 10 Mar. 2015, https://www.youtube.com/watch?v=Le-QMWdOMa-A.

27. "The House Always Wins | Tesla." Tesla, https://www.tesla.com/blog/house-always-wins. Accessed 16 Jan. 2023.

28. University of California Television (UCTV). The Atlantic Meets the Pacific: Exploring the Mind of an Entrepreneur - Elon Musk & James Fallows. YouTube, 2 Dec. 2011, https://www.youtube.com/watch?v=aRqfYBqPEQs.

29. Twitter, https://twitter.com/elonmusk/status/1311880821377175552?s=20&t=KF7VeRnELYAz-vM573Z9I6g. Accessed 16 Jan. 2023.

30. Twitter, https://twitter.com/elonmusk/status/1579094238998171648?s=20&t=JDx22txj_QiFtQmTiP-KeA. Accessed 16 Jan. 2023.

31. Elon Musk Videos Viral. Elon Musk "I Don't Give A Damn About Your Degree." YouTube, 10 Feb. 2018, https://www.youtube.com/watch?v=CQbKctnnA-Y.

32. Twitter, https://twitter.com/elonmusk/status/1580809382958227458. Accessed 17 Jan. 2023.

33. Twitter, https://twitter.com/elonmusk/status/1581092314176331776?s=20. Accessed 22 Apr. 2023.

34. Twitter, https://twitter.com/elonmusk/status/1581345747777179651?s=20&t=KF7VeRnELYAz-vM573Z9I6g. Accessed 16 Jan. 2023.

35. Lex Clips. Elon Musk: Advice for Young People | Lex Fridman Podcast Clips. YouTube, 30 Dec. 2021, https://www.youtube.com/watch?v=M-ZH3psUbfU.

IMPORTANCE OF BIRTH RATE

1. Twitter, https://twitter.com/elonmusk/status/1480564443629207557?s=20&t=KF7VeRnELYAz-vM573Z9I6g. Accessed 16 Jan. 2023.

2. Twitter, https://twitter.com/elonmusk/status/1566822635056599043?s=20&t=JDx22txj_QiFtQmTiP-KeA. Accessed 16 Jan. 2023.

3. Twitter, https://twitter.com/elonmusk/status/1533798671984119808?s=20&t=JDx22txj_QiFtQmTiP-KeA. Accessed 16 Jan. 2023.

4. Twitter, https://twitter.com/elonmusk/status/1469825142758989824?s=20&t=KF7VeRnELYAz-vM573Z9I6g. Accessed 16 Jan. 2023.

5. Elon Musk Videos. "We Are Going to Face a Demographic Implosion" - Elon Musk. YouTube, 15 July 2018, https://www.youtube.com/watch?v=ovAtU4i-5mDM.

6. Twitter, https://twitter.com/elonmusk/status/1283251937383550976?s=20&t=KF7VeRnELYAz-vM573Z9I6g. Accessed 16 Jan. 2023.

7. Elon Musk Videos Viral. Elon Musk's Full Interview at Code Conference. YouTube, 1 Apr. 2019, https://www.youtube.com/watch?v=lsO6gwLjhZE.

PREREQUISITE TO ATTRACT GREAT PEOPLE

1. muse.ai (c) 2022. Elon Musk on Dodging a Nervous Breakdown 2013. muse.ai, https://muse.ai/v/wT-d63RW-Elon-Musk-on-dodging-a-nervous-breakdown-2013. Accessed 6 May 2023.
2. Google Startups. Lessons on Leadership: Elon Musk + Sir Richard Branson. YouTube, 8 Aug. 2013, https://www.youtube.com/watch?v=Vy9y_YSpYxA.
3. Transcripts. "Tesla Motors (TSLA) Elon Reeve Musk on Q1 2016 Results - Earnings Call Transcript | Seeking Alpha." SeekingAlpha, Seeking Alpha, 5 May 2016, https://seekingalpha.com/article/3971543-tesla-motors-tsla-elon-reeve-musk-on-q1-2016-results-earnings-call-transcript.
4. Elon Musk and Peter Diamandis LIVE on $100M XPRIZE Carbon Removal. YouTube, 22 Apr. 2021, https://www.youtube.com/watch?v=BN88HPUm6j0.
5. "The Elon Musk Show - Media Centre." BBC, https://www.bbc.com/mediacentre/proginfo/2022/41/the-elon-musk-show. Accessed 18 Jan. 2023.
6. Elon Musk Talks Twitter, Tesla and How His Brain Works — Live at TED2022. YouTube, https://www.youtube.com/watch?v=cdZZpaB2kDM. Accessed 22 Apr. 2023.

GOLDEN AGE OF LEVERAGE

1. Recode. Elon Musk | Full Interview | Code Conference 2016. YouTube, 2 June 2016, https://www.youtube.com/watch?v=wsixsRI-Sz4.

2. Beach Bali Channel. Elon Musk with Nadiem Makarim Full Live Interview at Kampus Merdeka Festival | G20 Indonesia 2022. YouTube, 14 Nov. 2022, https://www.youtube.com/watch?v=Xp-fZcMOsdw.

3. Twitter, https://twitter.com/elonmusk/status/1419482326292172808?s=20&t=KF7VeRnELYAz-vM573Z9I6g. Accessed 16 Jan. 2023.

4. shazmosushi. Elon Musk's 2003 Stanford University Entrepreneurial Thought Leaders Lecture. YouTube, 12 July 2013, https://www.youtube.com/watch?v=afZ-TrfvB2AQ.

5. Vance, Ashlee. Elon Musk. Ecco, 2015.

6. Twitter, https://twitter.com/elonmusk/status/976414452106055680?s=20&t=ShQEaBiXB-Fis-vWiEH094A. Accessed 16 Jan. 2023.

DANGER OF AI

1. Brandalise, Caleb. Elon Musk - Full Interview : July 15, 2017 NGA Conference. YouTube, 16 July 2017, https://www.youtube.com/watch?v=PeKqlDURpf8.

2. Springer, Axel. Axel Springer Award 2020. YouTube, 1 Dec. 2020, https://www.youtube.com/watch?v=AF-2HXId2Xhg.

3. Brandalise, Caleb. Elon Musk - Full Interview : July 15, 2017 NGA Conference. YouTube, 16 July 2017, https://www.youtube.com/watch?v=PeKqlDURpf8.

4. Y Combinator. Elon Musk : How to Build the Future. YouTube, 15 Sept. 2016, https://www.youtube.com/watch?v=tnBQmEqBCY0.

5. Twitter, https://twitter.com/elonmusk/status/1598985189677740032?s=20&t=JDx22txj_QiFtQmTiP-KeA. Accessed 16 Jan. 2023.

6. Swisher, Kara. "Elon Musk: 'A.I. Doesn't Need to Hate Us to Destroy Us.'" www.nytimes.com, Sway, 28 Sept. 2020, https://www.nytimes.com/2020/09/28/opinion/sway-kara-swisher-elon-musk.html.

7. PowerfulJRE. Joe Rogan Experience #1169 - Elon Musk. YouTube, 7 Sept. 2018, https://www.youtube.com/watch?v=ycPr5-27vSI.

8. Yang, Jason. World Artificial Intelligence Conference 2019 / Tesla CEO Elon Talks with Alibaba Founder Jack. YouTube, 29 Aug. 2019, https://www.youtube.com/watch?v=IJlPVlqM8sw.

9. PowerfulJRE. Joe Rogan Experience #1169 - Elon Musk. YouTube, 7 Sept. 2018, https://www.youtube.com/watch?v=ycPr5-27vSI.

10. Training Program¬. How A.I. Deep Intelligence Can Start a War - Elon Musk. YouTube, 12 Nov. 2018, https://www.youtube.com/watch?v=al1JNBXPEkc.

11. Recode. Elon Musk | Full Interview | Code Conference 2016. YouTube, 2 June 2016, https://www.youtube.com/watch?v=wsixsRI-Sz4.

12. Twitter, https://twitter.com/elonmusk/status/1281121339584114691?s=20&t=KF7VeRnELYAz-vM573Z9I6g. Accessed 16 Jan. 2023.

13. PowerfulJRE. Joe Rogan Experience #1470 - Elon Musk. YouTube, 7 May 2020, https://www.youtube.com/watch?v=RcYjXbSJBN8.

AT THE END OF THE DAY, IT'S PEOPLE

1. Elon Musk Zone. "DON'T MAKE THIS MISTAKE!" — Elon Musk. YouTube, 26 May 2021, https://www.youtube.com/watch?v=jhVllI0tde8.
2. Elon Musk Videos Viral. Elon Musk "I Don't Give A Damn About Your Degree." YouTube, 10 Feb. 2018, https://www.youtube.com/watch?v=CQbKctnnA-Y.
3. Google Startups. Lessons on Leadership: Elon Musk + Sir Richard Branson. YouTube, 8 Aug. 2013, https://www.youtube.com/watch?v=Vy9y_YSpYxA.
4. BestVids. Elon's Strict No Asshole Policy #shorts. YouTube, 11 Oct. 2021, https://www.youtube.com/watch?v=OY-FZlvggVY.
5. "All Our Patent Are Belong To You | Tesla." Tesla, https://www.tesla.com/blog/all-our-patent-are-belong-you. Accessed 16 Jan. 2023.
6. PandoDaily. PandoMonthly: Fireside Chat With Elon Musk. YouTube, 17 July 2012, https://www.youtube.com/watch?v=uegOUmgKB4E.
7. Twitter, https://twitter.com/elonmusk/status/1591856396358025216?s=20&t=KF7VeRnELYAzvM573Z9I6g. Accessed 16 Jan. 2023.
8. Outcast Motivation. MIND BLOWING WORK ETHIC - Elon Musk Motivational Video. YouTube, 14 Nov. 2021, https://www.youtube.com/watch?v=-U5d-EdWouDY.
9. Elon Musk Talks Twitter, Tesla and How His Brain Works — Live at TED2022. YouTube, https://www.youtube.com/watch?v=cdZZpaB2kDM. Accessed 11 Feb. 2023.
10. Vance, Ashlee. Elon Musk. Ecco, 2015.

PROGRAM OR BE PROGRAMMED

1. Twitter, https://twitter.com/elonmusk/status/1465786605889892356?s=20&t=KF7VeRnELYAzvM573Z9I6g. Accessed 16 Jan. 2023.
2. Twitter, https://twitter.com/elonmusk/status/1465786605889892356?s=20&t=KF7VeRnELYAzvM573Z9I6g. Accessed 16 Jan. 2023.
3. Elon Musk Videos Viral. Elon Musk Gives Life Advice (2008). YouTube, 11 Mar. 2018, https://www.youtube.com/watch?v=9YY1riaTNUI.
4. Twitter, https://twitter.com/elonmusk/status/1584174386998697985?s=20&t=GOryLV-3Qsm-BuN_eTv8fMQ. Accessed 16 Jan. 2023.
5. "I Am Elon Musk, CEO/CTO of a Rocket Company, AMA! : IAmA." Reddit, https://www.reddit.com/r/IAmA/comments/2rgsan/i_am_elon_musk_ceocto_of_a_rocket_company_ama/. Accessed 16 Jan. 2023.
6. Business. "'Is Reading Important?'" - Elon Musk. YouTube, 22 Aug. 2021, https://www.youtube.com/watch?v=N--hz7XiZG8.
7. Business. "'Is Reading Important?'" - Elon Musk. YouTube, 22 Aug. 2021, https://www.youtube.com/watch?v=N--hz7XiZG8.
8. Vance, Ashlee. Elon Musk. Ecco, 2015.

THE NATURE OF SOCIAL MEDIA

1. Sense, Smart. Elon Musk: "DELETE Your Social Media NOW!" - Here's Why! YouTube, 14 Apr. 2022, https://www.youtube.com/watch?v=ponj6p2-iLQ.

2. PowerfulJRE. Joe Rogan Experience #1470 - Elon Musk. YouTube, 7 May 2020, https://www.youtube.com/watch?v=RcYjXbSJBN8.

3. Twitter, https://twitter.com/elonmusk/status/1568753942414168065?s=20&t=GOryLV-3QsmBuN_eTv8fMQ. Accessed 16 Jan. 2023.

4. Elon Musk Reveals His Knowledge on Aliens, Challenges Putin to UFC, and Predicts WW3. YouTube, 5 Aug. 2022, https://www.youtube.com/watch?v=fXS_gkWAIs0.

5. Elon Musk Talks Twitter, Tesla and How His Brain Works — Live at TED2022. YouTube, 14 Apr. 2022, https://www.youtube.com/watch?v=cdZZpaB2kDM.

6. Elon Musk Talks Twitter, Tesla and How His Brain Works — Live at TED2022. YouTube, 14 Apr. 2022, https://www.youtube.com/watch?v=cdZZpaB2kDM.

ON FEAR

1. Beach Bali Channel. Elon Musk with Nadiem Makarim Full Live Interview at Kampus Merdeka Festival | G20 Indonesia 2022. YouTube, 14 Nov. 2022, https://www.youtube.com/watch?v=Xp-fZcMOsdw.

2. Y Combinator. Elon Musk : How to Build the Future. YouTube, 15 Sept. 2016, https://www.youtube.com/watch?v=tnBQmEqBCY0.

3. Y Combinator. Elon Musk : How to Build the Future. YouTube, 15 Sept. 2016, https://www.youtube.com/watch?v=tnBQmEqBCY0.

4. Elon Musk Videos Viral. Elon Musk Gives Life Advice (2008). YouTube, 11 Mar. 2018, https://www.youtube.com/watch?v=9YY1riaTNUI.

5. Motive. Elon Musk - Challenge And How He Scaled Through. YouTube, 13 Nov. 2020, https://www.youtube.com/watch?v=gXjllXe66iQ.

6. Y Combinator. Elon Musk : How to Build the Future. YouTube, 15 Sept. 2016, https://www.youtube.com/watch?v=tnBQmEqBCY0.

7. Twitter, https://twitter.com/elonmusk/status/14610163 92916946947?s=20&t=iw-MdsDUIYhcmY5I02vuaA. Accessed 16 Jan. 2023.

8. Twitter, https://twitter.com/elonmusk/status/14940658 00482902030?s=20&t=iw-MdsDUIYhcmY5I02vuaA. Accessed 16 Jan. 2023.

9. Documentary. ELON MUSK: "Birthrate Might Be the Biggest Threat to the Future of Human Civilization". YouTube, 15 Apr. 2022, https://www.youtube.com/watch?v=2WX_mgnAFA0.

10. The Space Archive. RAW Elon Musk Interview from Air Warfare Symposium 2020. YouTube, 2 Mar. 2020, https://www.youtube.com/watch?v=sp8smJFaKYE.

11. Vance, Ashlee. Elon Musk. Ecco, 2015.

12. Vance, Ashlee. Elon Musk. Ecco, 2015.

13. Elon Musk Videos Viral. Elon Musk "I Don't Give A Damn About Your Degree." YouTube, 10 Feb. 2018, https://www.youtube.com/watch?v=CQbKctnnA-Y.

CHAOS AND ORDER

1. Elon Musk Videos Viral. Elon Musk's Full Interview at Code Conference. YouTube, 1 Apr. 2019, https://www.youtube.com/watch?v=lsO6gwLjhZE.

2. Politics, Space Policy. Elon Musk, Satellite 2020 Conference, Washington DC, March 9, 2020. YouTube, 24 Mar. 2020, https://www.youtube.com/watch?v=ywPqLCc9zBU.

3. Everyday Astronaut. A Conversation with Elon Musk about Starship. YouTube, 1 Oct. 2019, https://www.youtube.com/watch?v=cIQ36Kt7UVg.

4. Space Policy Politics. Elon Musk, Satellite 2020 Conference, Washington DC, March 9, 2020. YouTube, 24 Mar. 2020, https://www.youtube.com/watch?v=ywPqL-Cc9zBU.

5. Twitter, https://twitter.com/elonmusk/status/1426315521360896001?s=20&t=KF7VeRnELYAz-vM573Z9I6g. Accessed 16 Jan. 2023.

6. Oxford Languages and Google - English | Oxford Languages. https://languages.oup.com/google-dictionary-en/. Accessed 29 Apr. 2023.

7. All Elon Musk Videos. Elon Musk Talks Artificial Intelligence & Mars FutureFest - 2015. YouTube, 12 Sept. 2016, https://www.youtube.com/watch?v=X01ht-9MO0UQ

8. "Falcon 1: Start of an Era!" The Space Techie, 11 July 2021, https://www.thespacetechie.com/falcon-1-start-of-an-era/.

9. Berger, Brian. "Falcon 1 Failure Traced to a Busted Nut." Space.com, 19 July 2006, https://www.space.com/2643-falcon-1-failure-traced-busted-nut.html.

10. Bergin, Chris. "Space X's Falcon I Launch Success on Fourth Attempt." NASASpaceFlight.Com, 28 Sept. 2008, https://www.nasaspaceflight.com/2008/09/live-space-xs-falcon-i-to-make-fourth-attempt-for-success/.

THE NATURE OF ENTREPRENEURSHIP

1. Elon Musk Videos Viral. Elon Musk on How To Start A Business. YouTube, 5 Nov. 2017, https://www.youtube.com/watch?v=1RyuQR4qUgs.
2. Khan Academy. Elon Musk - CEO of Tesla Motors and SpaceX | Entrepreneurship | Khan Academy. YouTube, 22 Apr. 2013, https://www.youtube.com/watch?v=vDwzmJpI4io.
3. Khan Academy. Elon Musk - CEO of Tesla Motors and SpaceX | Entrepreneurship | Khan Academy. YouTube, 22 Apr. 2013, https://www.youtube.com/watch?v=vDwzmJpI4io.
4. Kong, Invest Hong. StartmeupHK Venture Forum - Elon Musk on Entreprencurship and Innovation. YouTube, 26 Jan. 2016, https://www.youtube.com/watch?v=pIRqB5iqWA8.
5. DraperTV. Eating Glass and Starting Up | Elon Musk (Iron Man). YouTube, 29 Jan. 2015, https://www.youtube.com/watch?v=yZlHbjxtECg.
6. Elon Musk | SXSW Live 2013 | SXSW ON. YouTube, 10 Mar. 2015, https://www.youtube.com/watch?v=Le-QMWdOMa-A.
7. Boes, Corrin. CHM Revolutionaries: An Evening with Elon Musk. YouTube, 24 Jan. 2018, https://www.youtube.com/watch?v=dQIQqOZqGIA.
8. Elon Musk Videos Viral. Elon Musk on How To Start A Business. YouTube, 5 Nov. 2017, https://www.youtube.com/watch?v=1RyuQR4qUgs.
9. California, Commonwealth Club. Jimmy Soni: The Inside Story of PayPal. YouTube, 10 Mar. 2022, https://www.youtube.com/watch?v=dvFEif0TWX4.

READ HISTORY

1. Carroll, Rory. "Elon Musk's Mission to Mars | Technology | The Guardian." The Guardian, 17 July 2013, https://www.theguardian.com/technology/2013/jul/17/elon-musk-mission-mars-spacex.
2. Université Paris 1 Panthéon-Sorbonne. Conversation Avec Elon Musk à Paris 1 Panthéon-Sorbonne. YouTube, 3 Dec. 2015, https://www.youtube.com/watch?v=BMskI6G9ty0.
3. Twitter, https://twitter.com/elonmusk/status/227291748798455809?s=20&t=KF7VeRnELYAzvM573Z9I6g. Accessed 16 Jan. 2023.
4. National Lab. ISSRDC 2015 - A Conversation with Elon Musk. YouTube, 8 July 2015, https://www.youtube.com/watch?v=ZmEg95wPiVU.
5. Highlights. Elon Musk and Tesla Engineers Answer Audience Questions at Tesla A.I. Day 2022. YouTube, 1 Oct. 2022, https://www.youtube.com/watch?v=Y4t-S0iVkFbg.
6. Twitter, https://twitter.com/elonmusk/status/1279875995516801024?s=20&t=KF7VeRnELYAzvM573Z9I6g. Accessed 16 Jan. 2023.
7. Twitter, https://twitter.com/elonmusk/status/228677717632098304?s=20&t=KF7VeRnELYAzvM573Z9I6g. Accessed 16 Jan. 2023.
8. Asimov, Isaac. Foundation. Bantam Books, 2004.
9. Twitter, https://twitter.com/elonmusk/status/1562340989775511552?s=20&t=JDx22txj_QiFtQmTiP-KeA. Accessed 16 Jan. 2023.

NO ONE IS 100% SELF-MADE

1. Elon Musk Videos Viral. Elon Musk & Bill Gates Talk Artificial Intelligence, China and Being Smart. YouTube, 18 Dec. 2018, https://www.youtube.com/watch?v=OqtOQj38ETo.

2. Twitter, https://twitter.com/elonmusk/status/1407868620680699908?s=20&t=J36-1beRE0fez1F9VH6zBg. Accessed 16 Jan. 2023.

3. Twitter, https://twitter.com/elonmusk/status/1473814525774336006?s=20&t=J36-1beRE0fez1F9VH6zBg. Accessed 16 Jan. 2023.

4. Twitter, https://twitter.com/elonmusk/status/1547332709025861632?s=20&t=J36-1beRE0fez1F9VH6zBg. Accessed 16 Jan. 2023.

5. Twitter, https://twitter.com/elonmusk/status/1545166492408328193?s=20&t=J36-1beRE0fez1F9VH6zBg. Accessed 16 Jan. 2023.

6. Twitter, https://twitter.com/elonmusk/status/1187114871231377408?s=20&t=J36-1beRE0fez1F9VH6zBg. Accessed 16 Jan. 2023.

7. Twitter, https://twitter.com/elonmusk/status/1575969637631565825?s=20&t=J36-1beRE0fez1F9VH6zBg. Accessed 16 Jan. 2023.

8. Twitter, https://twitter.com/elonmusk/status/8475942082193336705?s=20&t=J36-1beRE0fez1F9VH6zBg. Accessed 16 Jan. 2023.

9. Twitter, https://twitter.com/elonmusk/status/1583133885696987136?s=20&t=J36-1beRE0fez1F9VH6zBg. Accessed 16 Jan. 2023.

10. Twitter, https://twitter.com/elonmusk/status/13672737 22734911491?s=20&t=J36-1beRE0fez1F9VH6zBg. Accessed 16 Jan. 2023.

11. Twitter, https://twitter.com/elonmusk/status/97091468 1069039617?s=20&t=J36-1beRE0fez1F9VH6zBg. Accessed 16 Jan. 2023.

12. Twitter, https://twitter.com/elonmusk/status/1600932080237453312. Accessed 18 Jan. 2023.

13. Twitter, https://twitter.com/elonmusk/status/15170727 53475600385?s=20&t=J36-1beRE0fez1F9VH6zBg. Accessed 16 Jan. 2023.

ON INNOVATION

1. Everyday Astronaut. A Conversation with Elon Musk about Starship. YouTube, 1 Oct. 2019, https://www.youtube.com/watch?v=cIQ36Kt7UVg.

2. Butcher, Jack. "How to Create Value—Visualize Value." Visualize Value, Visualize Value, 16 Sept. 2021, https://visualizevalue.com/blogs/feed/how-to-create-value.

3. Elon Musk Videos. Elon Musk and Bill Gates Discuss A.I., Entrepreneurship and More 2015. YouTube, 25 Nov. 2015, https://www.youtube.com/watch?v=OLi0seDZoaI.

4. Tesla Founder and CEO Elon Musk Shares Energy Vision at 2015 EEI Annual Convention. YouTube, 11 June 2015, https://www.youtube.com/watch?v=UKT2tKmVk6g.

5. Elon Musk | SXSW Live 2013 | SXSW ON. YouTube, 10 Mar. 2015, https://www.youtube.com/watch?v=Le-QMWdOMa-A.

6. The Space Archive. RAW Elon Musk Interview from Air Warfare Symposium 2020. YouTube, 2 Mar. 2020, https://www.youtube.com/watch?v=sp8smJFaKYE.

7. The Space Archive. RAW Elon Musk Interview from Air Warfare Symposium 2020. YouTube, 2 Mar. 2020, https://www.youtube.com/watch?v=sp8smJFaKYE.

8. Kong, Invest Hong. StartmeupHK Venture Forum - Elon Musk on Entrepreneurship and Innovation. YouTube, 26 Jan. 2016, https://www.youtube.com/watch?v=pIRqB5iqWA8.

9. Elon Musk Videos Viral. Elon Musk on How To Start A Business. YouTube, 5 Nov. 2017, https://www.youtube.com/watch?v=1RyuQR4qUgs.

10. Swisher, Kara. "Elon Musk: 'A.I. Doesn't Need to Hate Us to Destroy Us.'" www.nytimes.com, Sway, 28 Sept. 2020, https://www.nytimes.com/2020/09/28/opinion/sway-kara-swisher-elon-musk.html.

11. PandoDaily. PandoMonthly: Fireside Chat With Elon Musk. YouTube, 17 July 2012, https://www.youtube.com/watch?v=uegOUmgKB4E.

12. Everyday Astronaut. A Conversation with Elon Musk about Starship. YouTube, 1 Oct. 2019, https://www.youtube.com/watch?v=cIQ36Kt7UVg.

13. NowThis News. Elon Musk Talks Space, Cars, and Video Games at E3 | NowThis. YouTube, 13 June 2019, https://www.youtube.com/watch?v=XHUCGN-DoWp4.

14. Channel 007. Elon Musk - MIT Aeronautics and Astronautics Department Interview. YouTube, 9 Aug. 2020, https://www.youtube.com/watch?v=qlClk-9G15i4.

15. The Space Archive. RAW Elon Musk Interview from Air Warfare Symposium 2020. YouTube, 2 Mar. 2020, https://www.youtube.com/watch?v=sp8smJFaKYE.

16. Heath, Alex. "Everything Elon Musk Told Twitter Employees in His First Company Meeting - The Verge." The Verge, The Verge, 11 Nov. 2022, https://www.theverge.com/2022/11/10/23452196/elon-musk-twitter-employee-meeting-q-and-a.

17. Twitter, https://twitter.com/elonmusk/status/1300098773348241408?s=20&t=KF7VeRnELYAzvM573Z9I6g. Accessed 16 Jan. 2023.

18. Chafkin, Max. "Entrepreneur of the Year, 2007: Elon Musk." Www.Inc.Com, https://www.inc.com/magazine/20071201/entrepreneur-of-the-year-elon-musk.html. Accessed 16 Jan. 2023.

19. Twitter, https://twitter.com/elonmusk/status/1590384919829962752?s=20&t=GOryLV-3Qsm-BuN_eTv8fMQ. Accessed 16 Jan. 2023.

20. World Government Summit. Mohammad Al Gergawi in a Conversation with Elon Musk during WGS17. YouTube, 15 Feb. 2017, https://www.youtube.com/watch?v=rCoFKUJ_8Yo.

21. Twitter, https://twitter.com/elonmusk/status/1584817409651007488?s=20&t=GOryLV-3Qsm-BuN_eTv8fMQ. Accessed 16 Jan. 2023.

22. Place, - Energy Meeting. Elon Musk, CEO of Tesla at ONS 2014. YouTube, 13 Nov. 2014, https://www.youtube.com/watch?v=0ZsVxSDB7NY.

23. Twitter, https://twitter.com/elonmusk/status/1536744900661755906?s=20&t=KF7VeRnELYAzvM573Z9I6g. Accessed 16 Jan. 2023.

24. The Space Archive. RAW Elon Musk Interview from Air Warfare Symposium 2020. YouTube, 2 Mar. 2020, https://www.youtube.com/watch?v=sp8smJFaKYE.

HORSE BLINDERS

1. Video, Every Elon Musk. Elon Musk Tells Tesla's History at 2016 Shareholders Meeting (2016.5.31). YouTube, 6 Mar. 2022, https://www.youtube.com/watch?v=C-LjN6IQmn8.
2. Invest Hong Kong. StartmeupHK Venture Forum - Elon Musk on Entrepreneurship and Innovation. YouTube, 26 Jan. 2016, https://www.youtube.com/watch?v=pIRqB5iqWA8.
3. Outcast Motivation. MIND BLOWING WORK ETHIC - Elon Musk Motivational Video. YouTube, 14 Nov. 2021, https://www.youtube.com/watch?v=-U5d-EdWouDY.
4. Twitter, https://twitter.com/elonmusk/status/1387172830094233601?s=20&t=KF7VeRnELYAz-vM573Z9I6g. Accessed 16 Jan. 2023.
5. Brownlee, Marques. Talking Tech with Elon Musk! YouTube, 18 Aug. 2018, https://www.youtube.com/watch?v=MevKTPN4ozw.
6. Brownlee, Marques. Talking Tech with Elon Musk! YouTube, 18 Aug. 2018, https://www.youtube.com/watch?v=MevKTPN4ozw.
7. "Musk Talks Early Troubles, Tesla's Future Video from Automotive News." Automotive News, 16 Jan. 2015, https://www.autonews.com/article/20150116/VIDEO/150119764/musk-talks-early-troubles-tesla-s-future.

8. Bemis, Tom. "Elon Musk Loves It When Tesla Competitors Do This - TheStreet." TheStreet, TheStreet, 10 Aug. 2022, https://www.thestreet.com/investing/elon-musk-loves-when-competitors-do-this.

9. Vance, Ashlee. Elon Musk. Ecco, 2015.

10. Vance, Ashlee. Elon Musk. Ecco, 2015.

11. Vance, Ashlee. Elon Musk. Ecco, 2015.

THE "BILLIONAIRE" THING

1. Elon Musk: A Future Worth Getting Excited about | TED | Tesla Texas Gigafactory Interview. YouTube, 18 Apr. 2022, https://www.youtube.com/watch?v=YRvf-00NooN8.

2. PowerfulJRE. Joe Rogan Experience #1470 - Elon Musk. YouTube, 7 May 2020, https://www.youtube.com/watch?v=RcYjXbSJBN8.

3. Twitter, https://twitter.com/elonmusk/status/1584539176997122048?s=20&t=JDx22txj_QiFtQmTiP-KeA. Accessed 16 Jan. 2023.

4. Clips. Why Elon Musk Is Selling His Possessions | Joe Rogan. YouTube, 7 May 2020, https://www.youtube.com/watch?v=1v--NMCwXqw.

5. PowerfulJRE. Joe Rogan Experience #1470 - Elon Musk. YouTube, 7 May 2020, https://www.youtube.com/watch?v=RcYjXbSJBN8.

6. Twitter, https://twitter.com/elonmusk/status/1016695490438619136?s=20&t=KF7VeRnELYAz-vM573Z9I6g. Accessed 16 Jan. 2023.

7. Twitter, https://twitter.com/elonmusk/status/1529961091656212514?s=20&t=KF7VeRnELYAz-vM573Z9I6g. Accessed 16 Jan. 2023.

8. Endelman, Judith. "Collecting Innovation Today." Thehenryford.Org, The Henry Ford, 26 June 2008, https://www.thehenryford.org/documents/default-source/default-document-library/transcript_musk_full-length.pdf?sfvrsn=f5722f01_0.
9. Investing, StateAlpha. Elon Musk 2015 Detriot Auto Show Full Interview. YouTube, 14 Jan. 2015, https://www.youtube.com/watch?v=LTbQFdyizGQ.
10. Twitter, https://twitter.com/elonmusk/status/1280597571459833863?s=20&t=KF7VeRnELYAzvM573Z9I6g. Accessed 16 Jan. 2023.
11. Twitter, https://twitter.com/elonmusk/status/1373507545315172357?s=20&t=KF7VeRnELYAzvM573Z9I6g. Accessed 16 Jan. 2023.
12. Third Row Tesla Podcast—Episode 7 - Elon Musk's Story - Director's Cut. YouTube, https://www.youtube.com/watch?v=J9oEc0wCQDE. Accessed 17 Jan. 2023.
13. PowerfulJRE. Joe Rogan Experience #1470 - Elon Musk. YouTube, 7 May 2020, https://www.youtube.com/watch?v=RcYjXbSJBN8.

THE FUTURE IS A BRANCHING SET OF PROBABILITIES

1. Swisher, Kara. "Elon Musk: 'A.I. Doesn't Need to Hate Us to Destroy Us.'" www.nytimes.com, Sway, 28 Sept. 2020, https://www.nytimes.com/2020/09/28/opinion/sway-kara-swisher-elon-musk.html.
2. Twitter, https://twitter.com/elonmusk/status/1007679828303024128?s=20&t=KF7VeRnELYAzvM573Z9I6g. Accessed 16 Jan. 2023.

3. Elon Musk: The Future We're Building -- and Boring |
    TED. YouTube, 3 May 2017, https://www.youtube.
    com/watch?v=zIwLWfaAg-8.
4. Swisher, Kara. "Elon Musk: 'A.I. Doesn't Need to Hate
    Us to Destroy Us.'" www.nytimes.com, Sway, 28 Sept.
    2020, https://www.nytimes.com/2020/09/28/opinion/
    sway-kara-swisher-elon-musk.html.
5. Elon Musk | SXSW Live 2013 | SXSW ON. YouTube,
    10 Mar. 2015, https://www.youtube.com/watch?v=Le-
    QMWdOMa-A.
6. Junod, Tom. "Elon Musk Interview - Elon Musk
    SpaceX Interview." Esquire, Esquire, 15 Nov. 2012,
    https://www.esquire.com/news-politics/a16681/
    elon-musk-interview-1212/.
7. Vance, Ashlee. Elon Musk. Ecco, 2015.
8. Stanford eCorner. Elon Musk: Elon Musk's Vision for
    the Future [Entire Talk]. YouTube, 11 Dec. 2015,
    https://www.youtube.com/watch?v=SVk1hb0ZOrE.
9. "Https://Twitter.Com/Elonmusk/Sta-
    tus/1205030950750412800?S=20&t=1UL8u6DrTy_
    TfMKl0jYrpA." Twitter, https://twitter.com/elonmusk/
    status/1205030950750412800?s=20&t=1UL8u6DrTy_
    TfMKl0jYrpA. Accessed 11 Feb. 2023.

ZOOMING OUT

1. Twitter, https://twitter.com/elonmusk/status/16010519
    61679171584?s=20&t=sOBGkjFaenGyYn-
    G6W1v0FQ. Accessed 10 Feb. 2023.
2. Twitter, https://twitter.com/elonmusk/sta-
    tus/1246995778746421248. Accessed 17 Jan. 2023.

3. Tesla, Third Row. Third Row Tesla Podcast—Episode 7 - Elon Musk's Story - Director's Cut. YouTube, 9 Feb. 2020, https://www.youtube.com/watch?v=J9oEc0wC-QDE.

4. Elon Musk: The Future We're Building -- and Boring | TED. YouTube, 3 May 2017, https://www.youtube.com/watch?v=zIwLWfaAg-8.

5. Twitter, https://twitter.com/elonmusk/status/1589644018727936001. Accessed 17 Jan. 2023.

6. Stanford eCorner. Elon Musk: Elon Musk's Vision for the Future [Entire Talk]. YouTube, 11 Dec. 2015, https://www.youtube.com/watch?v=SVk1hb0ZOrE.

7. Twitter, https://twitter.com/elonmusk/status/1387901003664699392. Accessed 17 Jan. 2023.

8. Space Policy Politics. Elon Musk, National Governors Association, July 15, 2017. YouTube, 16 July 2017, https://www.youtube.com/watch?v=b3lzFQANdHk.

9. Tesla. Tesla Battery Day. YouTube, 22 Sept. 2020, https://www.youtube.com/watch?v=l6T9xIeZTds.

10. Twitter, https://twitter.com/elonmusk/status/1588087419059916802. Accessed 17 Jan. 2023.

11. Twitter, https://twitter.com/elonmusk/status/1532267941512761346. Accessed 17 Jan. 2023.

12. SameerKDV. Full Speech of Elon Musk IAC 2017. YouTube, 29 Sept. 2017, https://www.youtube.com/watch?v=wM5D_SPBIv8.

13. "The Tesla Approach to Distributing and Servicing Cars | Tesla España." Tesla, https://www.tesla.com/es_ES/blog/tesla-approach-distributing-and-servicing-cars. Accessed 17 Jan. 2023.

14. Shahan, Zachary. "24 Tesla Shareholder Meeting Highlights - My Notes." CleanTechnica, 1 June 2016, https://cleantechnica.com/2016/05/31/tesla-shareholder-meeting-notes/.

15. The Mars Society. Elon Musk - 2020 Mars Society Virtual Convention. YouTube, 16 Oct. 2020, https://www.youtube.com/watch?v=y5Aw6WG4Dww.

16. Third Row Tesla. Episode 7 - Elon Musk's Story - Director's Cut. YouTube, 9 Feb. 2020, https://www.youtube.com/watch?v=J9oEc0wCQDE.

17. World Government Summit. Mohammad Al Gergawi in a Conversation with Elon Musk during WGS17. YouTube, 15 Feb. 2017, https://www.youtube.com/watch?v=rCoFKUJ_8Yo.

18. Online Harbour. WAIC 2019 - Elon Musk and Jack Ma - Artificial Intelligence Debate. YouTube, 2 Sept. 2019, https://www.youtube.com/watch?v=Vpx-2F6L8ST4.

19. Université Paris 1 Panthéon-Sorbonne. Conversation Avec Elon Musk à Paris 1 Panthéon-Sorbonne. YouTube, 3 Dec. 2015, https://www.youtube.com/watch?v=BMskI6G9ty0.

20. Twitter, https://twitter.com/elonmusk/status/1448874445150511114. Accessed 17 Jan. 2023.

21. Boustani, Maziyar. Elon Musk Interview AGU 2015 Conference San Francisco. YouTube, 16 Dec. 2015, https://www.youtube.com/watch?v=WwFa3nk1V0I.

22. "The Next, Next Thing—The Pennsylvania Gazette." The Pennsylvania Gazette, 1 Nov. 2008, https://thepenngazette.com/the-next-next-thing/.

23. "The Mission of Tesla | Tesla." Tesla, https://www.tesla.com/blog/mission-tesla. Accessed 17 Jan. 2023.

24. Fisbeck, Hagen. Elon Musk: AxelSpringer Award Talk with Questions from Other CEOs - 1.12.2020. You-Tube, 1 Dec. 2020, https://www.youtube.com/watch?v=heH1pWSqHN0.

25. Invest Yourself. Elon Musk: Recovering Rockets Is like Saving a $35M Pallet of Cash Falling from the Sky. YouTube, 27 Sept. 2020, https://www.youtube.com/watch?v=TOc6U6neUhg.

26. Space Policy Politics. Elon Musk, National Governors Association, July 15, 2017. YouTube, 16 July 2017, https://www.youtube.com/watch?v=b3lzEQANdHk.

27. Tesla's Solar City Acquisition Conference Call w/ Elon Musk [Full]. YouTube, 22 June 2016, https://www.youtube.com/watch?v=dm3q5ABMP14.

28. The Mind behind Tesla, SpaceX, SolarCity ... | Elon Musk. YouTube, 19 Mar. 2013, https://www.youtube.com/watch?v=IgKWPdJWuBQ.

29. Elon Musk | SXSW Live 2013 | SXSW ON. YouTube, 10 Mar. 2015, https://www.youtube.com/watch?v=Le-QMWdOMa-A.

30. Inc. A Conversation with Tesla CEO Elon Musk | Inc. Magazine. YouTube, 13 Nov. 2015, https://www.youtube.com/watch?v=Xcut1JfTMoM.

31. PowerfulJRE. Joe Rogan Experience #1470 - Elon Musk. YouTube, 7 May 2020, https://www.youtube.com/watch?v=RcYjXbSJBN8.

32. Twitter, https://twitter.com/elonmusk/status/1333972511524995072. Accessed 17 Jan. 2023.

33. Elon Musk | SXSW Live 2013 | SXSW ON. YouTube, 10 Mar. 2015, https://www.youtube.com/watch?v=Le-QMWdOMa-A.

34. Stanford eCorner. Elon Musk: Elon Musk's Vision for the Future [Entire Talk]. YouTube, 11 Dec. 2015, https://www.youtube.com/watch?v=SVk1hb0ZOrE.

35. Swisher, Kara. "Elon Musk: 'A.I. Doesn't Need to Hate Us to Destroy Us.'" www.nytimes.com, Sway, 28 Sept. 2020, https://www.nytimes.com/2020/09/28/opinion/sway-kara-swisher-elon-musk.html.

36. Stanford eCorner. Elon Musk: Elon Musk's Vision for the Future [Entire Talk]. YouTube, 11 Dec. 2015, https://www.youtube.com/watch?v=SVk1hb0ZOrE.

37. Tesla Founder and CEO Elon Musk Shares Energy Vision at 2015 EEI Annual Convention. YouTube, 11 June 2015, https://www.youtube.com/watch?v=UKT2tKmVk6g.

38. Twitter, https://twitter.com/elonmusk/status/1533616384747442176. Accessed 17 Jan. 2023.

39. Twitter, https://twitter.com/elonmusk/status/1330206139385044999. Accessed 17 Jan. 2023.

40. Place, - Energy Meeting. Elon Musk, CEO of Tesla at ONS 2014. YouTube, 13 Nov. 2014, https://www.youtube.com/watch?v=0ZsVxSDB7NY.

41. Stanford eCorner. Elon Musk: Elon Musk's Vision for the Future [Entire Talk]. YouTube, 11 Dec. 2015, https://www.youtube.com/watch?v=SVk1hb0ZOrE.

42. Recode. Elon Musk | Full Interview | Code Conference 2016. YouTube, 2 June 2016, https://www.youtube.com/watch?v=wsixsRI-Sz4.

43. "2015 AGU Fall Meeting." AGU - 2015 AGU Fall Meeting, https://agu.confex.com/agu/fm15/meetingapp.cgi/Session/11280. Accessed 17 Jan. 2023.

44. Twitter, https://twitter.com/elonmusk/status/699709623406702592. Accessed 17 Jan. 2023.

45. Twitter, https://twitter.com/elonmusk/status/1529968188410191879. Accessed 17 Jan. 2023.
46. Bhattacharya, Ananya. "5 Great Elon Musk Quotes on Innovation." Inc.Com, 20 Mar. 2015, https://www.inc.com/ananya-bhattacharya/5-elon-musk-quotes-about-innovation.html.
47. Twitter, https://twitter.com/elonmusk/status/1420901236862291968. Accessed 17 Jan. 2023.
48. States, Export-Import Bank of the United. 2014 Annual Conference| Discussion with Elon Musk. YouTube, 3 July 2017, https://www.youtube.com/watch?v=5ImZXTRyszE.
49. Twitter, https://twitter.com/elonmusk/status/1351056061759967240. Accessed 17 Jan. 2023.
50. Twitter, https://twitter.com/elonmusk/status/1293992502794448896. Accessed 17 Jan. 2023.
51. Twitter, https://twitter.com/elonmusk/status/1474405612662530077. Accessed 17 Jan. 2023.
52. Elon Musk at Tesla Shareholders Meeting 2016 -Part 2-. YouTube, https://www.youtube.com/watch?v=Ezu54pn5I4w. Accessed 18 Jan. 2023.
53. The Mind behind Tesla, SpaceX, SolarCity ... | Elon Musk. YouTube, 19 Mar. 2013, https://www.youtube.com/watch?v=IgKWPdJWuBQ.
54. Elon Musk Videos Viral. Elon Musk on Obama and Climate Change. YouTube, 24 May 2018, https://www.youtube.com/watch?v=Wz2X00FIfrc.
55. Twitter, https://twitter.com/elonmusk/status/1007766450256392192. Accessed 17 Jan. 2023.
56. Twitter, https://twitter.com/elonmusk/status/1363007438455074825. Accessed 17 Jan. 2023.

57. Twitter, https://twitter.com/elonmusk/status/1529645883280834561. Accessed 17 Jan. 2023.

58. Twitter, https://twitter.com/elonmusk/status/1525631880279822337. Accessed 17 Jan. 2023.

59. Place, - Energy Meeting. Elon Musk, CEO of Tesla at ONS 2014. YouTube, 13 Nov. 2014, https://www.youtube.com/watch?v=0ZsVxSDB7NY.

60. Tesla. Tesla Battery Day. YouTube, 22 Sept. 2020, https://www.youtube.com/watch?v=l6T9xIeZTds.

61. Twitter, https://twitter.com/elonmusk/status/1349977642708168704. Accessed 17 Jan. 2023.

62. Twitter, https://twitter.com/elonmusk/status/1472701397049225232. Accessed 17 Jan. 2023.

63. PowerfulJRE. Joe Rogan Experience #1470 - Elon Musk. YouTube, 7 May 2020, https://www.youtube.com/watch?v=RcYjXbSJBN8.

64. Twitter, https://twitter.com/elonmusk/status/1588081971221053440. Accessed 17 Jan. 2023.

65. Cellan-Jones, Rory. Elon Musk - the Full BBC Interview. YouTube, 13 Jan. 2016, https://www.youtube.com/watch?v=0871VJfvD1c.

66. Twitter, https://twitter.com/elonmusk/status/1533606056756137985. Accessed 17 Jan. 2023.

67. The App Store Chronicle. LOST: Elon Musk, Before Paypal. YouTube, 24 Sept. 2014, https://www.youtube.com/watch?v=ZHKT3yxYvDQ.

68. Stanford eCorner. Elon Musk: Elon Musk's Vision for the Future [Entire Talk]. YouTube, 11 Dec. 2015, https://www.youtube.com/watch?v=SVk1hb0ZOrE.

69. Khan Academy. Elon Musk - CEO of Tesla Motors and SpaceX | Entrepreneurship | Khan Academy. YouTube, 22 Apr. 2013, https://www.youtube.com/watch?v=-vDwzmJpI4io.

70. How to not give a f*ck. Elon Musk on Overcoming His First Fear. YouTube, 14 Oct. 2013, https://www.youtube.com/watch?v=suD1aBwwZfU.

71. Twitter, https://twitter.com/elonmusk/status/1598758363650719756. Accessed 17 Jan. 2023.

72. Twitter, https://twitter.com/elonmusk/status/1598383918276755457. Accessed 17 Jan. 2023.

73. Twitter, https://twitter.com/elonmusk/status/1597629846611726336. Accessed 17 Jan. 2023.

74. Twitter, https://twitter.com/elonmusk/status/1596083744728928257. Accessed 17 Jan. 2023.

75. Twitter, https://twitter.com/elonmusk/status/1595454820407980032. Accessed 17 Jan. 2023.

76. Twitter, https://twitter.com/elonmusk/status/1594732430933782528. Accessed 17 Jan. 2023.

77. Twitter, https://twitter.com/elonmusk/status/1594729874031247361. Accessed 17 Jan. 2023.

78. Twitter, https://twitter.com/elonmusk/status/1347126794172948483. Accessed 17 Jan. 2023.

79. Twitter, https://twitter.com/elonmusk/status/1593759933773643776. Accessed 17 Jan. 2023.

80. Twitter, https://twitter.com/elonmusk/status/1593300520168398848. Accessed 17 Jan. 2023.

81. Twitter, https://twitter.com/elonmusk/status/1593264249731620864. Accessed 17 Jan. 2023.

82. Twitter, https://twitter.com/elonmusk/status/1591850617462738946. Accessed 17 Jan. 2023.

83. Twitter, https://twitter.com/elonmusk/status/1589448512382857218. Accessed 17 Jan. 2023.
84. Twitter, https://twitter.com/elonmusk/status/1589403131770974208. Accessed 17 Jan. 2023.
85. Twitter, https://twitter.com/elonmusk/status/1584527241400442886. Accessed 17 Jan. 2023.
86. Twitter, https://twitter.com/elonmusk/status/1583149077792858112. Accessed 17 Jan. 2023.
87. Twitter, https://twitter.com/elonmusk/status/1582005061583978496. Accessed 17 Jan. 2023.
88. Twitter, https://twitter.com/elonmusk/status/1581036916597657601. Accessed 17 Jan. 2023.
89. Twitter, https://twitter.com/elonmusk/status/1523622304592187392. Accessed 17 Jan. 2023.
90. Twitter, https://twitter.com/elonmusk/status/1577880686282919937. Accessed 17 Jan. 2023.
91. Twitter, https://twitter.com/elonmusk/status/1545485800833372160. Accessed 17 Jan. 2023.
92. Twitter, https://twitter.com/elonmusk/status/1573165011484413952. Accessed 17 Jan. 2023.
93. Twitter, https://twitter.com/elonmusk/status/1571346394811711488. Accessed 17 Jan. 2023.
94. Twitter, https://twitter.com/elonmusk/status/1569417348179759107. Accessed 17 Jan. 2023.
95. Twitter, https://twitter.com/elonmusk/status/1568017475325014016. Accessed 17 Jan. 2023.
96. Twitter, https://twitter.com/elonmusk/status/1568012443233779712. Accessed 17 Jan. 2023.
97. Twitter, https://twitter.com/elonmusk/status/1567783902273540100. Accessed 17 Jan. 2023.
98. Twitter, https://twitter.com/elonmusk/status/1567789461899038721. Accessed 17 Jan. 2023.

99. Twitter, https://twitter.com/elonmusk/status/1563292201043431424. Accessed 17 Jan. 2023.
100. Twitter, https://twitter.com/elonmusk/status/1547927887734456322. Accessed 17 Jan. 2023.
101. Anderson, Chris. "Elon Musk's Mission to Mars." Wired. www.wired.com, https://www.wired.com/2012/10/ff-elon-musk-qa/. Accessed 17 Jan. 2023.
102. Twitter, https://twitter.com/elonmusk/status/1536555363453095937. Accessed 17 Jan. 2023.
103. Twitter, https://twitter.com/elonmusk/status/1535733409083011073. Accessed 18 Jan. 2023.
104. Twitter, https://twitter.com/elonmusk/status/1533103614885089281. Accessed 17 Jan. 2023.
105. Twitter, https://twitter.com/elonmusk/status/1532728628378746885. Accessed 17 Jan. 2023.
106. shazmosushi. Elon Musk's 2003 Stanford University Entrepreneurial Thought Leaders Lecture. YouTube, 12 July 2013, https://www.youtube.com/watch?v=afZ-TrfvB2AQ.
107. Daum, Meghan. "Elon Musk, CEO of Tesla and SpaceX, Wants to Change How (and Where) Humans Live | Vogue." Vogue, Vogue, 21 Sept. 2015, https://www.vogue.com/article/elon-musk-profile-entrepreneur-spacex-tesla-motors.
108. World Government Summit. Mohammad Al Gergawi in a Conversation with Elon Musk during WGS17. YouTube, 15 Feb. 2017, https://www.youtube.com/watch?v=rCoFKUJ_8Yo.
109. Gulik, Greg. Elon Musk Interviewed by Fareed Zakaria CNN. YouTube, 26 Nov. 2013, https://www.youtube.com/watch?v=zet-X_7MG_Q.

110. Twitter, https://twitter.com/elonmusk/status/1580957341200941064. Accessed 17 Jan. 2023.
111. Twitter, https://twitter.com/elonmusk/status/14922273 28386154509?s=20&t=iw-MdsDUIYhcmY5I02vuaA. Accessed 16 Jan. 2023.
112. The Space Archive. RAW Elon Musk Interview from Air Warfare Symposium 2020. YouTube, 2 Mar. 2020, https://www.youtube.com/watch?v=sp8smJFaKYE.
113. Tesla Motors (TSLA) Elon Reeve Musk on Q1 2016 Results - Earnings Call Transcript | Seeking Alpha. https://seekingalpha.com/article/3971543-tesla-motors-tsla-elon-reeve-musk-on-q1-2016-results-earnings-call-transcript. Accessed 17 Jan. 2023.
114. The Mars Society. Elon Musk - 2020 Mars Society Virtual Convention. YouTube, 16 Oct. 2020, https://www.youtube.com/watch?v=y5Aw6WG4Dww.
115. Twitter, https://twitter.com/elonmusk/status/810108760010043392. Accessed 17 Jan. 2023.
116. Invest Hong Kong. StartmeupHK Venture Forum - Elon Musk on Entrepreneurship and Innovation. YouTube, 26 Jan. 2016, https://www.youtube.com/watch?v=pIRqB5iqWA8.

THE MEANING OF LIFE

1. Twitter, https://twitter.com/elonmusk/status/1510510978286428163. Accessed 17 Jan. 2023.
2. Twitter, https://twitter.com/elonmusk/status/1552317587694010368. Accessed 17 Jan. 2023.
3. Joe Rogan Experience #1470 - Elon Musk. YouTube, https://www.youtube.com/watch?v=RcYjXbSJBN8. Accessed 17 Jan. 2023.

4. Third Row Tesla. Third Row Tesla Podcast—Episode 7
- Elon Musk's Story - Director's Cut. YouTube, 9 Feb.
2020, https://www.youtube.com/watch?v=J9oEc0wC-
QDE.
5. Tesla Owners Silicon Valley. Elon Musk on Life, The
Universe and Everything: Interview Part 2. YouTube,
14 June 2022, https://www.youtube.com/
watch?v=iHmSrK238vI

ELON MUSK BOOK RECOMENDATIONS

1. Twitter, https://twitter.com/elonmusk/sta-
   tus/143171132814671872?s=20. Accessed 6
   June 2023.
2. Twitter, https://twitter.com/elonmusk/sta-
   tus/154313189079777280?s=20. Accessed 6
   June 2023.
3. Twitter, https://twitter.com/elonmusk/sta-
   tus/1664812106460323843?s=20. Accessed 6
   June 2023.
4. Twitter, https://twitter.com/elonmusk/sta-
   tus/542004522298535936?s=20. Accessed 6
   June 2023.
5. Elon Musk: SpaceX, Mars, Tesla Autopilot, Self-Driv-
   ing, Robotics, and AI | Lex Fridman Podcast #252.
   www.youtube.com, https://www.youtube.com/
   watch?v=DxREm3s1scA. Accessed 6 June 2023.
6. Twitter, https://twitter.com/elonmusk/sta-
   tus/1230293973673136129?s=20. Accessed 6
   June 2023.

7. Twitter, https://twitter.com/elonmusk/status/1014752854333009921?s=20. Accessed 6 June 2023.

8. Twitter, https://twitter.com/elonmusk/status/1181656686236508160?s=20. Accessed 6 June 2023.

9. Twitter, https://twitter.com/elonmusk/status/198113448628981760?s=20. Accessed 6 June 2023.

10. Twitter, https://twitter.com/elonmusk/status/902452162625544193?s=20. Accessed 6 June 2023.

11. Twitter, https://twitter.com/elonmusk/status/1380480918243090433?s=20. Accessed 6 June 2023.

12. Twitter, https://twitter.com/elonmusk/status/149435658115612672?s=20. Accessed 6 June 2023.

13. Twitter, https://twitter.com/elonmusk/status/1479182795796717571?s=20. Accessed 6 June 2023.

14. Twitter, https://twitter.com/elonmusk/status/338399341641342976?s=20. Accessed 6 June 2023.

15. Twitter, https://twitter.com/elonmusk/status/198113448628981760?s=20. Accessed 6 June 2023.

16. Twitter, https://twitter.com/elonmusk/status/1647119228376416258?s=20. Accessed 6 June 2023.

17. Twitter, https://twitter.com/elonmusk/status/496010572333580289?s=20. Accessed 6 June 2023.

18. Twitter, https://twitter.com/elonmusk/status/1205807718969139200?s=20. Accessed 6 June 2023. AND Twitter, https://twitter.com/elonmusk/status/579504748014907393?s=20. Accessed 6 June 2023.

19. Highly Recommended Books By Elon Musk. www.youtube.com, https://www.youtube.com/watch?v=e-boFcjgMpvs. Accessed 6 June 2023.

20. Twitter, https://twitter.com/elonmusk/status/1455264663810232331?s=20. Accessed 6 June 2023.

21. Twitter, https://twitter.com/clonmusk/status/1279875995516801024?s=20. Accessed 6 June 2023.

22. Twitter, https://twitter.com/elonmusk/status/495759307346952192?s=20. Accessed 6 June 2023.

23. Twitter, https://twitter.com/elonmusk/status/742120520678703105?s=20. Accessed 6 June 2023.

24. Twitter, https://twitter.com/elonmusk/status/584978236053917697?s=20. Accessed 6 June 2023.

25. Highly Recommended Books By Elon Musk. www.youtube.com, https://www.youtube.com/watch?v=e-boFcjgMpvs. Accessed 6 June 2023.

26. Twitter, https://twitter.com/elonmusk/status/1567139578166890506?s=20. Accessed 6 June 2023.

27. Twitter, https://twitter.com/elonmusk/status/609215984499605504?s=20. Accessed 6 June 2023.
28. Twitter, https://twitter.com/elonmusk/status/1653075645138710528?s=20. Accessed 6 June 2023.
29. Twitter, https://twitter.com/elonmusk/status/198113448628981760?s=20. Accessed 6 June 2023.
30. Twitter, https://twitter.com/elonmusk/status/1473824879820615680?s=20. Accessed 6 June 2023.
31. Twitter, https://twitter.com/elonmusk/status/1494349659111833600?s=20. Accessed 6 June 2023.
32. Twitter, https://twitter.com/elonmusk/status/1628084060101783559?s=20. Accessed 6 June 2023.
33. Twitter, https://twitter.com/elonmusk/status/1554335028313718784?s=20. Accessed 6 June 2023.
34. Twitter, https://twitter.com/elonmusk/status/1008101573472354304?s=20. Accessed 6 June 2023.

ABOUT THE AUTHOR

Mack Moderie is a builder. He left university in 2020 and started a solar panel cleaning business that same year.

A year into building that business, he ventured into the social media space. He has grown two larger accounts. One is The Knowledge Archivist (@KnowledgeArchiv) which is essentially a collection of distilled, useful knowledge from biographies.

The other account is, of course, Musk University. Mack believes there is a lot of potential to provide value to others through that account and has started by writing *The Hitchhiker's Guide to Mars*.

Mack is also helping build a health community with Mikhaila Fuller (Jordan Peterson's daughter). The community is focused on healing mood and autoimmune related disorders through diet. The diet consists of ruminant meat, salt, and water. The diet was coined 'the Lion Diet' by Mikhaila back in 2021. Mikhaila reversed her severe arthritis on the diet and Mack relieved himself of symptoms of multiple sclerosis. The community has seen unbelievable health recoveries. Mack believes deeply in the potential of this diet.

Made in United States
Troutdale, OR
06/27/2023

10829906R00236